Dreaming Without Wings

by

RHONDA RHOSE

WingSpan Press

Published in the United States and the United Kingdom
by WingSpan Press, Livermore, CA

The WingSpan name, logo and colophon are the trademarks of
WingSpan Publishing.

ISBN 978-1-59594-598-3 (pbk.)
ISBN 978-1-59594-920-2 (ebk.)

First edition 2016

Printed in the United States of America

www.wingspanpress.com

Library of Congress Control Number: 2016958181

1 2 3 4 5 6 7 8 9 10

ACKNOWLEDGEMENTS

A lot of personal growth went into the writing of this book. It has been finished no less than four times, and then re-configured so as to make the concepts new to me easier to comprehend. During this time, I had the support of family and friends who never failed to encourage, understand and even try to imagine a world where the voice of spirit is busy correcting my thoughts. While distracting at first, it was a process almost unnoticeable after the first year or two, but to be a support team to one in this awkward condition deserves special appreciation.

A special thank you goes to my soul family, those invisible beings that allowed me to experience a premature opening of the 3rd eye and the crown chakra so that I might learn enough about our soul's existence that I can allow myself the luxury of knowing that I am only a speck of our universe, but still an integral part of the whole.

My most heart-felt love and gratitude go to my family, Ken, Angie and Brian Biritz. Ken, this exploration would not have been possible without your financial backing, since you are my constant in numbers and were still willing to give up my status as *employed*. Angie, your intellectual/emotional common sense and your ability to transcend the ceilings I gave up on are a constant sense of amazement and inspiration. Brian, your heart-centered ability to hear your mind talk to you insures me that I am on the right road. For that and for your willingness to just be, I thank you.

To my brother, Steven VanOrman, I offer the greatest thanks for allowing me to test my theories with his personal situations, including his own ability to hear when the vibration hits the magic mark on the love barometer. To my mother, Lorna VanOrman, thank you for enduring the role of mother when you might easily have given up. And thank you, Deane Gemmell, for the work we did together.

During the initial power-washing swirlys, unconditional support was always available from my three Marys; Mary-Rocha-Smith, Mary Elizabeth Perez, and Laughing Mary Holewyczynski. You were all consistently encouraging for me during my efforts to restructure the me that I am today. To Donna Mullins and The Crystal Connection, Thank You. Donna's support of my abilities ensured that I found my worth during my most faltering moments. To Gale and Rita Hokenson, thanks for believing in me probably more than I deserve; your support kept me pushing through with a book that might never have made it to the light of day.

Patty Reddy, thanks for the never-ending help with cover design and artwork as well as help in just being a friend. Terri Hall, thanks for the edit when things were so raw they probably hurt your eyes and ears, but you supported me nevertheless. Tracy Stutzman, you are another of my laughing-rocks of sanity. You showed up at just the right moment and continue to do so. You are all friends of a divine status. I love you all and couldn't have pushed through without your hearts and your questions – the questions keep me motivated.

You are all more valuable to me than you could even know.

Peace Be,

"There is a side of you that wants more from us and we can give you that and your library of past times once you arrive on our side of mind."

The Watcher, Ecknoreial

TABLE OF CONTENTS

CHAPTER 1

DREAMING WITHOUT WINGS

I knew I was through the worst of it and yet here I was being jerked awake again and making my way through the house in the dead of night, with a muscle spasm that radiated from my upper thigh all the way through my calf. That cramp had me stomping around like a pirate with a wooden leg and had seismic activity that surely registered a seven on the Richter scale. The spasm didn't let up for at least five minutes, but when it finally released its hold on me I stood there in a wet night gown as sweaty and nauseous as if I had just given birth to twins. Earlier that day, during a perfunctory trip to the grocery store, I prayed *not to faint* as I made my way to the checkout line. I held fast to a grocery cart that had now become my make-shift walker while the light headedness and gnawing anxiety threatened to pull me under. In both instances my mind flashed the all too familiar sign into the ON position: SWIRLY IN PROCESS. I knew the procedure. There was a reinforcement going on down under, just to make sure I didn't return to an old way of dealing or feeling.

"Tell me again, please," I prayed to the air above my head, "just *how* is this supposed to help anything?"

My answer was already there; I just had to find the right channel to connect with my spirit entourage. You see, there is a divine intercession that keeps us awake at night and holds our memory hostage, one designed to awaken the super-hero components of our mind in a way that allows us access to newer and better ways of problem solving and of attracting the desired circumstances into our lives. I have experienced an unusual format of study in this area in that my professors were the soul guides we use to orchestrate our lives. They have allowed me access to the closed doorways of our inner world, doorways that include dimensions of possibility that will be normal capability once we clear the foggy residue stored in our subconscious memory banks. Itching, sneezing and seizing, we are clawing our way up out of the dirty basement of our stored negativity and finding our way, ever so slowly, to the top of our inner mountain.

Conversations with a guide are becoming far more commonplace now that the veil is thinning and our consciousness evolving, but the guidance we hear is not always of the highest vibration, depending on our state of mind. I am an intuitive consultant with an internal superciliousness that is hopefully flushing its way out of my system. Being supercilious implies a sense of haughty sarcasm and I'll be the first to admit that my thoughts take a turn towards sassy arrogance when I am in a defensive mode. *Super-silly-us*, all hanging on for dear life to our individual sense of superiority and all because we haven't yet recognized that we are good enough just as we are. What I didn't know was that those well-hidden, snarky little thoughts were a big deal in terms of what was holding me back. There is usually a raised eyebrow associated with *super.silly.us* and I used to get that a lot from my spirit-professors. I have the unusual distinction of being able to hear my invisible entourage 24/7. They have explained that the invasion of my privacy was so I could learn how our minds work and how to maximize our true consciousness potential. I have learned somewhere along the way that spirit guides are simply the voice of our soul-mind, which equates to our inner guidance, or higher self. When I asked my guides why they call me Rhose, which isn't my name, by the way, they said, "*Because sometimes you're smelly. We are here to help you with that.*" Suffice it to say, hearing spirit guides has its advantages as well as pitfalls, but I know one thing for sure, when they seem supercilious, I'm the one off track again.

At one point I could have classified myself as a New Age junkie since I stayed a little high on my sense of self-importance. Insert *your* raised eyebrow here. A lot of the belief systems I held will naturally take you to that point if you follow them without realizing where you are in terms of your own lessons. As a psychic reader, I was full of wisdom and great advice and at dispensing just the right verbal fix to take you to your own personal high. Then all that changed when somewhere up on high, much higher than my personal high, it was decided that I needed to flush my subconscious mind of all the unresolved fear sleeping in there. That included and began with my inflated sense of self.

The swirly that held me captive brought an implosion to so much of my spiritual belief system that I practically had to rebuild from ground zero. The shift left me feeling isolated and bereft of all the pat answers I carried with me. All of my past lives debunked, and realizing I was no one special in the overall scheme of things, I finally realized that what I had really held onto were my fears, my incomplete sense of self. Masked in neat little boxes, I kept my insecurity gift-wrapped in magical soliloquies, complete with genies in bottles to grant my secret wishes – illusionary as they were. How I could be so full of faith and yet wonder if there was a god that actually heard my prayers is something I can never fully explain, but that's about the whole of it, or the hole in it, I'm not sure which.

Like my own imploded philosophical paradigm, my intuitive abilities kept me face to face with a continuous stream of clients moving through their own belief system crashes, sometimes in regards to their religious ideals, but more often than not, there was a common element of clearing the negativity from a perception or behavior that seemed to lay at the root of their discomforts. I have come to truly believe that the rationalizations that arise as a camouflaging attempt to hide our insecurities are by far the hardest to pinpoint and resolve. The layers of subterfuge we feed ourselves become so comfortable that we forget the truth that hides just beneath the surface. As for myself, I really thought I had all the answers. I was just topping off my folder of accomplishments when the rug was pulled out from under me – the magic carpet that organized all my spiritual understandings from reincarnation to ghost-tracking. I couldn't find my owner's manual; where do I go when my new age beliefs crash too?

My worlds collided the day that I began to hear my spirit entourage on a continuous basis. Not just reverberating with the word I most needed to tune into my client or my working-overtime-again-curiosity, but with input into every thought I had, and not always welcome input at that. It was kind of like learning to diagram a sentence again only this time I was getting the hidden meaning of every word that crossed my vocal mind. The beginning of my lessons in understanding the workings of my subconscious mind entailed several classes on random thoughts and their origins. It seems that all the unresolved gunk in our subconscious really influences the way we see things. It plays far too big a part in creating our perceptions of us and our relationship to the world around us.

Normally I am quite chatty, I suppose, but I had come to find myself becoming increasingly quiet as circumstances around me caused me to shut down somewhat. For that reason, I developed my own conversations within and far too many of them were spent defending myself from some imagined slight or in scenarios that hadn't even happened yet. Since that realization, I have spent the last several years taking the tour of my intuitive mind with these guides I have come to call my invisible entourage. As my self-centered beliefs crumbled, one by one, I began to ask them for the truth; not just the truth I most needed for my own personal development, not the truth that the masses hold to, but the truth of how it really works, how it resonates from the god-point of creation down to the physical dimensions and into my personal world. At this point all I can say is to be careful of what you ask for, because in this instance I most certainly came face to face with my flawed sense of self, a self neatly hidden beneath layers of intricate masking devices that kept me from wanting to deconstruct the last few layers that would ultimately expose me to my own truth.

My guides make me work for the truth. They won't just hand it to me like you would imagine. Contrary to what you might think, my life isn't one big psychic reading from the other side, nor is it one big ongoing class in whatever I want to know. You could say my entourage and I are an interactive system; kind of a *WE;* I have to keep dancing to earn a high enough score to get my reward points – which are hopefully the answers to some of my questions in a truth based format and not a symbolic representation of whatever lesson I am waddling

4

through. The crux here is that spirit is quite capable of answering us or communicating with us in a very understandable and simplistic format. When the verbiage is awkward or requires decoding, or even deals with a minute amount of symbolism, there is distortion present and that is a sure sign that we, as seekers of spirit awareness, require a higher rating on our love barometers. The answers we get will be matched in frequency to the love, or it's polar opposite – fear – in the questions.

The amount of truth I get depends on the quality of my intentions and the barometer reading on my love-meter. That disturbance in the force, it's usually just me slipping out of a love vibration and getting another supercilious eyebrow. That has remained my goal though, to get the truth. I have learned one thing in all this; at some level every thought we have is, in essence, asking the universe for something, and based on the cause and effect of our lives, the information we get from spirit is based on the degree of emotional maturity present in our requests. If I want the truth, I had darn-well better be coming from a place of high integrity sans the ego-high or my truth isn't quite crystalline in nature and neither will the information be that spirit sends my way. That little realization makes me wonder about things like Jehovah smiting villages and other divine historical happenings. Curiously though, I find that as my perceptions clear themselves of my defense mechanisms, things become easier and I get more of the truth-based understanding I am searching for.

During psychic readings I try to keep the invisible faction focused on the client and not me. A lot of it boils down to something quite different than my original understanding; they are not looking for an outlet to speak, as you may have been told; they are members of our higher-self-team, our soul, and they are really here to help us with our personal lessons, first and foremost, in finding that elusive love vibration, a frequency that transcends conflict of any kind, conflict within ourselves as well as with those around us. Those lessons can include erroneous information designed to shift a client's mind-set long enough to provide some barometric healing. Rest assured, if you are on the receiving end of an incorrect message, your inner guidance will let you know – one way or the other. In fact, the invisible faction has explained that they will always supply some mis-information just so we don't become overly dependent on their input in our lives. This complicated and misunderstood aspect of a psychic reading applies both to the client and the reader, which means I really need to take a minute to clear my mind of its supercilious trap doors before I tap into the etheric airspace over my head.

In a nutshell, if I can hold that love vibration up there, that means moving past my own personal insecurities well enough that my intentions are truly motivating towards being of service to others, and not to shine on as the best reader in town, then guide-speak can come through without the distortion caused by my fog-of-immaturity. But just in case I'm feeling a little shaky in the self-worth department, I can use the tarot too. Tarot works the same way, but for me personally, it is a back-up plan. The cards are just tools to help me to shift my focus in case my ego trips me up; they buy me a little time to clean up my mind. For the most part though, I have learned to circumvent that side of me that wants more, more, more – at least during a reading.

At this point we've come to an agreement, my invisible entourage and I. Giving readings is my work and I have made the grade sufficiently well that they are cooperative when it comes to helping others through these shifting tides of change; otherwise they are only here to help me clean up my own act. Sometimes they speak through me; I feel them merge with my mind and then they take over operation of my voice box. That's called channeling, - and NO, I am not in a trance. I have complete control and can stop them at any time. Sometimes I do the talking as they pass along the information I need. The truth is they can give me the material in a split second. I take a fraction of a second to ask silently if I have it right and they confirm or correct as necessary. How to read for a client is always a bit of a conundrum in that they are usually seeking the thrill of the channeling and oftentimes that is why they have come to see me. A certain high arises from knowing there is a spirit-being focused on you and actually involved in conversation with you, BUT the real truth is that I can pass along your messages with far more clarity and will also provide the wisdom necessary for living in our three-dimensional world in a much simpler and effective format. Guide-speak is rather scripture-esqe and stems from concepts slightly removed from our version of life and love. Fortunately for me, I have had over twenty years experience in guide-speak translations, both in their verbiage and concepts. I know when they are telling you something wrong so you will shift your focus and when they are alluding to something good coming but fail to mention that you may have to work for it. A chat with guide-speak usually creates enough of a sense of magic for the client that it is necessary to remind said client that the experience of other-worldly communication is not a magic wand; it is still necessary to do your homework and take the required action. The job you want IS out there but you will have to meet your invisible faction half-way and type the resume and pound the pavement to find it, at least until we have flushed enough of the fear in our belief systems to ride the right wave of energy, the one that matches the perfect circumstances to our desires. That wave exists but it exists a few chakras above our activation point, or in simpler terms, we're a few degrees too far down on our love meters when we operate from a point of wishing and hoping without really *knowing and moving* on the end-result-possibility.

As far as me and my life, what I get from guide-speak will vary, depending on which emotional playlist I am riding. Still, I persist in asking for the truth in how it all works. I don't always get it the first few times, I am still learning how to hold that love vibration up there, but there does come a point where, if the truth is of benefit to the whole and if I am coming from a place of honesty with self in regards to the origins of my desires, they will give me the truth of how things work between us and them in a simplified enough format that I can pass it along. During my first few swirlys, the intense subconscious power washings that cause mega-leg cramps during the night, they began to point out layers of fear that clouded my interpretations of the spiritual philosophies I held to so tightly. Once I began to deconstruct my spiritual paradigm, and replace the fear-based aspects with love, something I really didn't understand as well as I do now, the worn and dirty windows began to fall out of my palace of perceptions and replace themselves with stained glass in colors brighter than I had ever thought

7

possible.

The real truth is a vast and expanding concept. As I piece together my new window of beliefs, I have learned that no matter how you shake it down, truth must always mold to fit your unique perceptive window, a window that changes, a window that stays in constant motion. I thought I already knew it all, but I have added another layer or two in understanding how our individual thoughts, words and deeds, as well as our intentions, mold the matter that we create for ourselves, our perceptions of reality. That is exactly how our unique perceptive windows are formed; we ride a wave of energy that all too often incorporates our sense of what stinks into the making of the world around us.

I have learned so much that here I am again, ready to write this book, to explain how it all works, and not sure where to begin…

*"So here **we** are; your entourage…"*

"You want them to hear from us? They will."

*"We want **you** to push through,"*

"Until you've moved where you want to,"

"And then we'll come in,"

"And offer our assistance again."

"Rhyming is our sign that things are not quite right. When you listen for the rhyme, you lose the integrity of the words while trying to hold the energy pattern of the verse. That is where you are at this space and time."

As official guide-speak translator, let me just say that they are talking about our need to break out of old blueprints of behavior and viewpoints. We can become so wrapped up in the patterns of the rhythm and the rhyme that we lose the real meaning of our words. We tend to allow ourselves to look back at how it worked before and use that as the template for moving through something new. The message here is to learn to think outside the box of what was or has been true in the past; to do so will offer far more in possibility and opportunity.

"You are your own best friend these days and that is how it will need to be until you can find your identity in individuality and integrity. You are wondering why we say it that way. We are the first to admit that you are the one who preaches this message to those you counsel and

you believe you understand exactly what that entails, but you are only looking at one perceptive layer at a time."

Say what? I know this usually comes up in readings where the client is vulnerable to losing sense of self in order to hold onto a relationship. Does this mean I am losing my sense of self by clinging to my *spirit guide* relationship?

"You are."

Ouch.

"We are now your friends in that we will assist you in your belief systems so that you can unfold the truth of the rhose in a way that reveals that the belief systems you abide by will hinder your sense of self until you can release your expectations of writing a good book and not embarrassing us…"

As I read these words I see that this last statement meant so much more than I realized the first time they sent it my way. They have, indeed, hindered me in writing this book. I might have given up, but there is a memory in that statement to remind me that maybe this is something worth pursuing. A very long time ago, an old friend brought me a *message*. The timing was perfect so it must have carried a prophetic knowing of what was to come for me. At least I thought that was how synchronicity worked…

I was reading a rather innovative book at the time and had some questions as to the authenticity of the material, much like I usually do. There is that side of me that is pseudo-skeptical and believing in magic all at the same time. Without divulging the details of the entire message, she gave me one incredibly profound riddle…

"On page 142 is a very specific message for you…"

New oracle that she was, my friend was anxious; she hadn't provided such specific information before and didn't have a copy of the book to check it out so she offered the message to me with some trepidation. I made haste to find the book and open it to page 142. The page was blank …

Except for one sentence:

"Write a good book, and don't embarrass us."

I took it as the sign I needed, and still, all these years later it serves to remind me that I still want to write the book.

"Push through. Push through the veil that keeps you from moving ahead."

Alright. I have started and stopped this book more times than I care to admit, even to myself. One thing that I could always do was write. I would muddle through the first sentence or two and then point my mind in the right direction and abracadabra - I was in the flow. The river's current usually took me exactly where I wanted to go, with only one concern: would I have time to finish before I said everything I had to say?

I have a lot more time now, if only I hadn't lost my faux-sense of surety. The darnedest thing is that my new awareness carries so much more now in terms of understanding how it all works, but I can't seem to find the right way to pass it along. I now have this conscious connection to spirit and to my subconscious, the *collective* that is often referred to as the *unconscious*, so it should be simple enough to put my message into a book that even Dick, Jane and Sally could understand. It should be, *"Write, Sally, write,"* but it's more like, *"See Rhose run.* So here I sit rambling and hoping the rug stays stationary for a while yet. I am trying to re-pattern the subconscious programming that stole my ability to feel the flow of my words, and my own entourage did it! You're going to want to understand the *why* of that because it is happening to many of us right now. Have you recently experienced the loss of your thoughts or the perfect word right there in mid-sentence? Has your heart taken on the beat of an internal drum for no apparent reason? How's your anxiety level lately?

"We are holding your subconscious mind hostage these days until you are able to discern when you are acting out of a fear-based belief system or when you are believing that we are the answer to your life's questions. We are and we are not."

"We are your friends when you need us and we are your guardians when you feel lost but we will always monitor your word, thought and deed, tempered by your motivational desires, so that you can find your way without our input."

"You can turn the Beatles off now so that you can focus on what we are saying. You love the Beatles more than us and we love that about

you. If you can find your own way in this world, we will be happier with you than when you want us to show you the way."

Hmmm, yes; the swirly-meisters did take my writing ability from me but they also taught me to sing. When I was a little kid I was sure I was an undiscovered prodigy just waiting for my big break with Mr. Microphone, but it only took a few *"shut-up, Rhondas"* to end that dream. In retrospect, I suppose I have never pushed through too hard if it wasn't easy. And being heard was not always easy. But that's the thing; writing *was* easy.

Unbeknown to me, I was learning to put myself in a higher vibration with my spirit-taught singing lessons, not only because I enjoyed them but because I was symbolically learning to harmonize from an energy playlist of higher resonance. First they told me that I was hard of hearing middle tones and that was why I wasn't getting the results I wanted. So they fixed my hearing. I felt nothing but I was suddenly able to hear the whole melody, which makes it so much easier to find the notes when you want to sing. I had no idea I was missing half the material. I was later to understand that the reason I had lost some of my hearing ability was because I was unable to handle certain levels of stress brought on by the normal circumstances of life. Due to feeling left out, I was tending to bond with others in ways unbecoming to a love vibration in attempts to fit into the group mold. Translation: over-identification with anyone singing the blues or rapping to the faults of you-know-who.

Then I discovered that I didn't have to sing down there with Cher just because her notes were the ones I could hear well. I can sing that low but it isn't my natural range. When I learned to be comfortable with my own voice, 2nd soprano was so much easier. I found my comfort a couple octaves higher. It's not high, but it's a lot more like Olivia Newton-John than Cher. I had to be able to hear the melody from that higher range to be able to sing it, but until they corrected my hearing, I couldn't hear what I was missing so I didn't miss it. Nor did I have a clue as to how symbolic that whole scenario was going to become in my life.

"Why?"

Why???

"Because your heart needed some quiet time. Your singing wasn't an issue, your ability to hear too much of what was around you was a problem."

My fear of not bonding with the group created a glitch in my perceptions that caused me to ride a resentful wave of energy that stayed lower to the ground, so to speak, than I would have travelled had I been able to release my truth as a means of motivational energy. These things happen in a world wrought with fears. It's kind of like saying I was a couple octaves lower to physical survival than up and flying with angels.

So moving on, I sing because it clears my mind and it helps me to find a higher wave of vibration. Music really works when my goal is to push my perceptive window upward. I get help with my voice too. If I am trying to find the sound, they take control and do it for me until I get the hang of it. It takes a little confidence; I have to sing and trust they will find the notes for me, but it works. I have to ask them for help though because one of my lessons is to recognize my desires, which, for me, begins with taking note of what I want, something I hadn't learned to do. And they will even add what sounds like back-up singing along with my voice if I ask for some additional power. I am not a belter and they are getting me comfortable with that, with a more relaxed style, but if I must belt; they will do it with me. I'm still a pragmatist though; I'm not good enough nor am I sufficiently inspired to make a career of it. I don't know if anyone could hear them when they do the back-up but...

"Yes and no. When we power your voice you would notice an additional harmonizing factor that one person could not do alone but you never let anyone hear you. That is sad for us but your family is not interested in hearing you sing. Your son does know you can sing and he listens when he is in the mood."

Oh. I believe I may have actually been struck speechless with that. I had no idea my son *ever* listened to me...

But lately I have been wondering more about harmonizing and they are working with me on that. They take my voice and locate the appropriate notes while I take note of how they work together. It is really exciting for me. If you have studied music, it would be no big deal, but for me it's complete magic!

"Why?"

Why???

"Let's look deeper…"

Well, let me look at that a minute; because you have made it impossible for me to write and I am embarrassed by my lack of literary output. But when we are working on music, it feels like I have your cooperation. Also, it makes me feel good about me and everything around me.

Oh, I see, I am still feeling the need to prove myself with my ability to hear you.

But *WE* digress, so I was working on a book for all the wrong reasons when it happened; when I started dancing the swirly. I was quite sure I was all systems go, endowed with the confidence of my writing ability and gifted with the magic of an invisible speaker ready to do the work for me. I picked my topic and sat down at the computer - and sat – and stared at the screen – and waited; I even came back the next day to try again, but nothing ever happened except a sinking feeling that I was never going to get anywhere with my new-found abilities. It was the beginning and the ending of my channeling-author career. Finally, all I heard was *"you are done with this book; it is not for you."*

That was about the time my WE had begun a continuous stream of chatter in my direction. I wasn't sure if I should listen or start transcribing everything they said. I was sure I was on the precipice of something big and I was right. They pushed me *right* over the cliff. By way of explanation, all they said was, *"we will strip you of your defenses until you are defenseless…and rebuild from a higher point of awareness."*

'Seems kinda' cold for beings of an angelic vibration…

And believe me; it was cold for a while. It was the beginning of my dark night of the soul; stripping me of my defenses. I didn't even know I had them. But now, as I let them go, I find my awareness expanding, my life becoming easier and richer, *and* my behind is not quite as expansive as it was, but it's still super-sized.

I am now in the process of rebuilding my own belief systems so I have a tendency to present things as *food for thought*. I'm not as sure of myself as I used to be but at least now I know that I was never all that sure of myself. In some of the ways that I was most secure, I was wrong. I had developed a false platform of self-structure that consisted of a lot of *"holier than thous"* (oh, thanks, guys). But the truth is, those defenses covered up a lot of uncertainty.

And since then, my invisible entourage has indeed made it very hard for me to write. There has been a steady stream of mishaps all connected to my writing that have created a gaping hole in my belief that I can do this thing that was once so natural for me. All my life I felt the pull to write a book but I never had the inspiring material to make it move. Finally, I had my inspiration and suddenly I could no longer string five words together well enough to hold my own attention. I was re-programmed in a way that made it hard to believe I could even write a grocery list.

"Push through. You know you can do this but we made it hard to move ahead without some additional support in the ways of self. You know you have the ability but you needed the reasons to be of a more supportive-to-the-cause intention than to explore and expound on the magic of WE."

I am ignoring that; some of it is simply because I wanted their magic more than doing it myself and some is true in other ways that are better understood later, including that of an embarrassing little desire of wanting to shine on as a chosen one. Some of the *whys* of stripping me of my writing ability (was writing a defense?) are unknown to me but I can explain parts of the phenomenon. I used to joke that I was a better writer than speaker. More often than not, I can speak well if I am comfortable with the topic and endeared to those around me, but I had increasingly found myself in situations where I was becoming more and more silent. I only spoke my truth when the going was easy. Since the shattering of my spiritual perceptive window, I have learned a thing or two as to the why of that. I was out of balance in the realms of communication. There was a kernel of fear that required removal from my communicative window. Somehow I had never learned to speak openly unless I was sure it was 110% safe.

I used to wonder if there were lessons for small talk. When I lost my privacy, I got those lessons. I literally heard my guides instruct me as to the topics and the questions to open a dialogue. Since I could no longer write worth a darn, I was forced, ever so-not-gently to open up in face-to-face situations. I was sure I was missing part of the communication gene. I couldn't help myself, just look at the people around me. They had so much to say that I couldn't get a word in edgewise, so I just gave up. I fooled myself into believing that what I had to say wasn't important enough to say out loud, that because I so much wanted to be heard, I believed that they only wanted to be heard as well, and so I made myself indispensable by listening.

I would tend to listen oh-so-well but offer little input unless I was absolutely sure that the other person really wanted my words of wisdom. A sincere *I understand* became my mantra. For the most part, I put my most natural responses away for later, when my instant replay button kicked on and I began to wish I had responded to some imagined slight, or defended some other unresolved issue in my vast treasure-trove of misaligned beliefs.

Too many *shut-ups* can do that to you. You come away with a misperception that your words have no validity. That means your thoughts have no validity. That means you have no validity on some unresolved, subconscious level. And sometimes all people really want *is* to be heard, but if you're asking to be heard then there might be an implied contract that says you are also agreeing to listen. If we could just learn to listen to each other with our minds opened, to seek the similarities rather than the differences, we would have a much wider arc of possibility in this world. That was something I had to work through in a way that had me risk being vulnerable in asking to be heard. But I did it enough that maybe I can finally write again.

"Your voice is not your issue, your words are. Why? We are asking you to explain it..."

Right. When the instant replay kicks on in your head, the unresolved stuff is looking for an outlet to right itself; to resolve things to a point of peace within. That may or may not be possible, depending on how you are looking at them.

By divine design, everything, even the most minute thought, is energy and energy naturally flows towards good, or God. That movement is Love. So in divine mind, your thoughts are the beginning of shaping your reality – almost. Those random thoughts can really trip you up. They come from somewhere and usually they are coming from an unresolved issue wafting around in your subconscious. They are meant to travel along the river of love, but when they are open-ended in a way that makes you uncomfortable at your inner core, where the true measure of love resides, they tend to bond with the other unresolved issues stored in your subconscious warehouse of remorseful memories. Once the instant replay begins, you have just changed your inner-channel to the tune of tainted love, and the instant replay will continue to kick in until all life experiences are resolved to love. The good news is that restoring the circumstances of your life to a memory of peace from a point of highest integrity will erase the negative energy wave from your Akashic recording for this life. The swirly is the process being used to clear us of this karmic residue. It may sound impossible to correct all of it but there is a divine intervention in place to help us make it manageable.

For me, what was happening was that my mind conjured up too many unresolved scenarios based upon my agreeable, listening approach to things where I never acknowledged to myself that I might have been hurt by a remark or that I might have disagreed strongly with another's opinion. My thoughts were becoming *"clouded with judgments and with defense mechanisms still in place but trying hard to discard"* (thanks again, guys). Point being, my thoughts were contaminated with anger and hurt, all because I didn't address them in a resolving way right there when they were happening. And PS, that doesn't mean you confront the other party with their error in perception; it means you address your own insecurity in discovering why the remark had the power to bother you in the first place. In a true state of emotional maturity, if we are accidently hurt by another, we would seek to understand our own area of weakness rather than place blame on another. If someone's remarks or perceptions have the power to hurt us, we are riding a wave of reality that is contaminated with our own fear. Once we clear enough fear to ride a higher wave, the same remarks would pass by us unnoticed. That is a difficult concept for us at this point in time and one of the things to be repaired while our higher soul energies orchestrate a flushing of the fear for each of us, one based on our individual needs.

In truth, you would not know me to be full of supercilious snark. I was good at keeping my wayward thoughts under the surface and genuinely felt the warmth and compassion I displayed outwardly. But later my inner thoughts, which were where I spent too much time, fell out of love. That causes a rift in the subconscious programming that serves more than we realize to push us forward in everyday life. I had to clean up my thoughts and stop the desire to prove myself of value. And to clean up my thoughts, I had to learn to put them out there in an honest and yet conforming way. I had to learn to speak my truth and let go of the fear that kept me from doing so, all while never harming another being, even with my random thoughts.

Before my dance with the swirlys, all you had to do was mention the word *subconscious* and I lost interest. I am typically a fairly deep thinker and not afraid of subjectivity, but delving into a concept that always comes off as a dark and dirty basement kicks my mind back into the aloof state, at least on the surface, and underneath, in my raw-thought-stage it might be something more like: "Did my hair go flat yet? I hope I don't have roots as gray as hers. At least my skunk stripe is white and not mouse gray." And then I imagine myself twenty years younger and fifty pounds lighter and compare that mental image to the innocent by-standing lady who brought up the term subconscious – just to make sure I am not aging prematurely, of course.

That's what I mean by cleaning up my thoughts. That poor, fictitious lady that wanted to talk about the subconscious - something I was unsure about – suffered – in the ethers – my supercilious judgments. My discomfort with the topic sent my subconscious searching for something similar in feeling to assist me in my small talk. It took my unsure feeling and connected the dots with my unsure feelings about aging, which are really just subterfuge because my real diffidence is my weight, but it's just too hard to say to myself, 'damn, I'm fatter than her too."

Feeling unsure was my motivating force, which stems from my raw emotional reaction. My lack of confidence in discussing the term *subconscious* attached itself to stored memories of similar emotional discord, which, at that point, unfortunately orchestrated a faux-therapeutic scenario based on my fear of not being sexually attractive. In a love vibration, our thoughts should do no harm. My thoughts at that point were based in fear when they began their journey through space and time. Soon they would unfold in mold and assault my sense of smell the next time I stood in front of the bathroom mirror to check out the wrinkles around my eyes and mouth, or more honestly, the spare tire around my hips. Our minds are shifting and we are becoming capable of so much more than we were before, so there you have it; Creation 101 – how to culture mold spores in your steamy bathroom, complete with an easy button.

Not only is that how energy works, but our physical senses are being held hostage by our guides too, so they can make sure we know exactly what we're creating when we call the guy turning left without signaling an asshole. 'Been noticing any surprising smells lately? Here I am talking about spirit guides holding our subconscious minds hostage and telling you that they will even turn your sensitivity knob up so high that you can't hide even your most secret feelings. By now you're probably wondering if possibly I haven't quite yet found that mind I lost.

Oh, and by the way, one of biggest gauges spirit uses in determining where you are on the love-barometer is in measuring those raw emotional reactions, not the eloquent, redesigned responses we send out to our audience but the raw 'oh crap' thought that manifested before we had time to wrap it in pretty layers of organic tissue. That's what the second chakra is really about; that *seat of emotion* refers to our raw emotional reactions to the world around us. The *sex* part refers to how we interact with those around us in terms of processing those raw emotional reactions. In our divine design, that raw emotion will, for a while, become the force that propels us forward. The whole point being that we are to train those raw reactions to rise an octave or two higher. To do that, we have to have our hearing repaired, so to speak, so we can come face to face with the hidden melody we have been humming.

Here's the thing though, the repairs just might keep you awake all night with a good dose of listening to your own darn thoughts...

CHAPTER 2

WHERE IS MY SUBCONSCIOUS?

When my guides started spewing a continuous stream of chatter in my direction; they were playing a couple different roles; a small tidbit they neglected to mention. As spirit guides, they are what is referred to in metaphysics as the *superconscious*. They are my connection to the higher realms, they are the voice of my soul and beyond if necessary, but that's the thing – our soul is sufficiently constructed to handle anything we encounter while in our physical dimension, at least at this stage of our mental evolution. Superconscious activity is what we're looking for when we pray and meditate, when we ask for miracles, when we search our dreams for hidden meanings. And just so you know, superconscious doesn't work well with supercilious. Being supercilious indicates that the flow of my conscious mind has gone slightly off-course and is defending my I-me-mine instead of working for the good of the whole.

The tour of my intuitive self became incredibly complicated when my superconscious took on that supercilious tone. I can now say I am not so haughty in my approach to metaphysical belief systems but my road to realization was not easy. I would imagine that my ability to internalize so well was a big factor; otherwise I might have been drugged by doctors and dragged around by the people I was putting down in my mind. It had become such an habitual format that I wasn't really consciously aware of my own frames of reference. And please understand, I wasn't running continuous tirades and rants through my mind, just having intermittent thoughts about why I might be better at something or less wrong about things than someone else. It doesn't take much to drop the barometric rating of our love barometers.

What I eventually learned was that my superconscious guides would take off their super-hero costumes and articulate my every thought for me in a way that made it impossible to ignore. They also magnified it with a well-chosen word in just the right spot to let me know something was rotten in Denmark again and somehow what was rotten was coming around to me. Have you noticed any slimy verbiage creeping into your thoughts every once in a while? The kind that makes you not like yourself quite so much…

For me, the term subconscious conjured up visions of ghoulish characters playing leap frog and having sword fights. When my superconscious, super-heroes finally enlisted my help in repairing the broken sump pump of my subconscious, I really didn't know what to expect. What is this mysterious part of my mind that seems to have a mind of its own and how can I possibly fix it?

Well, I finally understand it enough that I think I can pass it along in a way that will help us want to clean our symbolic basements. I have a good reason for believing that you will want to know about this; I see hundreds of clients and have become convinced that we're all – every one of us with sufficient emotional stability to handle it – having our fears flushed. I'm not the only one with superconscious activity surfacing; every one of us has a higher self up there clearing and cleaning the way for a ride up the elevator of insight where we can see through a brighter window. The only difference is that in many cases your soul self will use more of the subconscious mind to speak to you. That only means that you cannot hear the message consciously, but you're getting it loud and clear – subliminally. That is exactly where those funny little short-lived earaches or bouts of tinnitus are coming from; they clue you in that what you're hearing from the subconscious realm is slightly off in some way. And let me tell you, when your superconscious goes supercilious, you know there's a swirly with your name on it somewhere.

Our subconscious mind contains a recording of our life – from every nuance of a thought to every spark of vanity that crosses our inability to see ourselves in all of our beauty. That is our long term memory bank. Every word we have ever read is in there and every chocolate chip we even thought about is in there with its own personal identity.

The problem isn't the chocolate chips, it's the way we file these memories. Point in case, why are my chocolate chip friends filed under guilt? You won't have to do a doctoral thesis to understand this and make corrections; it's as simple as recognizing a love-based motivation and applying it to everything in your life. Ok, so it's not easy either, but I promise it's not rocket science, and at least no one grades you on it or uses it to withhold your next pay raise. You are the only one involved; you and your soul family.

Imagine having every thought, every word and every twinge of a desire recorded for posterity; it's not a pretty sight. It's like knowing the whole neighborhood is watching every time you look backward in the full-length mirror to see if you're still too fat to wear your skinny jeans. As a long-time student of metaphysics, I have known since my early twenties that this Akasha thing existed, a secret dimension that holds our life-records, and I have been mildly aware that every poison dart my mind blows is out there on some great cosmic DVD, but who really gives a darn? I mean, my Akasha et su Akasha and all that but nobody really cares enough about my twinkling thoughts and assorted other farts to push the play button. Do they???

Well, that's the thing. Our subconscious holds our Akashic recording for this lifetime. It is that secret dimension that recorded every smell we thought we detected. The Akasha is a dimension of possibility that exists in the spirit realms, simply meaning we have easier access to it from there then we do from the realm of the physical. I am going to bore you for a minute in an effort to make this as simple as possible – because it really is. There is no need to make metaphysical concepts out to be magical mystery tours.

We are physical beings. That means we are born into a physical body here on earth, also known as the world of form. That also means that we are spirit beings, sparks of mind, who have agreed to minimize our thinking capacity to the point that we can learn more from a very individualized perspective. In spirit we tend to exist in groups that ride waves of energy based on similar interests and philosophical paradigms. As humans, we are exploring the realm of possibility from the viewpoint of the individual mindset. This allows us a deeper understanding of how we operate when in fear, meaning our motivations stem from the negative end of the emotional spectrum, because we are unsure of our connectedness to a higher power. All negativity stems from a fear of survival, something that does not exist in the immortal realm of spirit. In the world of form we agree to be born in the physical world and to learn from the perceptive windows of the human. Our bodies are made of earth, again the physical, but our minds are the soul part, the spirit. We are a spark of divine consciousness that will evolve through eternity, in one form or another, depending on our choices.

When we are in the realm of spirit, our consciousness is far more expansive than now. We can do so much more and all because we are one big, beautiful, brilliant mind that can tap into all the other beautiful, brilliant minds out there simply by desiring to do so. We can travel to other planets without space ships, check out their skinny jean looks and be back here all in a nano-second. All those different dimensions you hear about that exist outside of us; they are really just additional realms of possibility within our own mind when we are back in the land of no limitations, that of spirit, but some of that possibility is becoming available to us now and that is what this book is all about, the shifting of our conscious minds.

So the Akasha is an actual dimension or capability of our mind that exists in spirit – a.k.a. – beyond our normal reach while in the physical unless higher self does the magic for us. It is really the source of a lot of the confusion we have about time not being real. Time exists in the dimensions of spirit too; they just don't use our clocks or the Gregorian calendar; the focus is on the present. The reason the Akasha is so confusing in regards to time is because it has a fast forward button and a rewind feature. It also contains layers of possibility in your present depending on the energy wave or channel you're surfing at that moment, which is partially determined by your perceptions of the world around you. For the moment, we are more interested in the fast forward and rewind buttons. You can pick a time, any time, buzz back there and relive a minute or two with Attila the Hun – just long enough to save his soul and feel like a hero – and come back to your now, without the super-hero costume but feeling better about yourself, without even knowing why. You didn't change history; you simply inserted yourself into your own graphic novel in a scenario that revolved around the original Akashic-life-recording of Attila and his entourage.

That's part of what the Akasha is, a big 'ole library of time. In it resides the sum total of all of our subconscious mind-recordings from every single lifetime all playing together off one big holographic flash drive, including our soul interactions. If you need to understand what might have happened had you done something differently, your higher self could take you to that recording and allow you to move through an alternate reality to make the necessary point. You didn't change what originally happened but you did go through an alternate reality-route as a tool to heal or better facilitate your understanding. An alternate reality would indicate you were riding a different wave of resonance, a different channel or frequency, so to speak. It's kinda' that touched by an angel thing…

The cool thing is the Akasha fast-forwards too. That doesn't mean your future is predestined; it just means that based on the patterns of where you are now, there is a probable prediction for the future. That's where prophesy comes from. It's like throwing behavior pattern coordinates into a GPS and getting your future destination, based on the energy wave you're riding at that moment. Actually, that is the reason for prophesy – so you can change the coordinates that you don't want. You don't have to wait for Armageddon so things can get better; just change your playlist channel, the wave of energy you're riding, your GPS coordinates, so you go in a different direction. Since higher self is the queen of multi-tasking, she can monitor every whiff I have of psychosomatic odors and still play the Akasha of high probability all around me, in every direction, just to see what's around the next bend. That way, if a train on my path is about to de-rail, she can re-route me without my even knowing it. A big sale on handbags will usually do the trick; I won't even have to know there was danger.

So once I realized the guides were monitoring my very-likely-immediate-future and hopefully helping me decide which direction to turn, I came to the decision that it might be wise to ease off on the garbage that went into my subconscious recording, meaning my snarky thoughts and other assorted defenses, so that I might find my destination a little easier. It isn't a punishment scenario but I know now that the more I stay in a love vibration, the less I have to deal with in the way of resolving my own subterfuge. You know, garbage in, garbage out...

The subconscious is really a giant storehouse of information, at least in terms of what we're most dealing with in this book. There is also a portion of your own reasoning consciousness in there and it – which is another side of you – is always trying to retrieve whatever information you might be able to use to make peace with whatever you're experiencing at the moment. The problem lies with the mental and emotional maturity level of our reasoning subconscious. Because our vibration of mass consciousness is overly incorporated with fear, with negative emotional reactions that have become defense mechanisms, our subconscious reasoning is not as wise or as honest as it should be. Stay with me here; this is really simple to understand, I promise.

The term *dimensional shift* indicates that there are some more advanced portions of our mind seeking to reunite with the limited mind we are using in our day-to-day life. That's what that 11:11 thing is all about. How many times have you noticed those numbers in the last few years? Reuniting with these other avenues of conscious ability amps up our awareness and makes us more like the spirit magicians we want to be. That is what is meant when you hear that the veil is thinning. It simply means your own consciousness is moving through the fog of fear to reunite with portions of its vast and magnificent self so it can move beyond the abilities and limitations we have now, while we are still here in the physical.

Let me see if I can make this less tedious. In writing this book, finding where I left off can keep me re-reading and tweaking until I lose my feeling of progress. Instead of beginning by re-reading my work, I wish I could just jump in and write while knowing that some part of my mind will keep things cohesively connected and on track. My subconscious mind works a lot like that and once I shift enough of the negativity out of my vision, I will be able to remember exactly where I left off and where I wanted to go. But for now it bonds with too many other unfinished topics in my subconscious and keeps me worried about where to go next. The book is unfinished and therefore requires resolution. I worry about the words being awkward so I keep readjusting the flow so that it sounds like a casual conversation rather than reading your homework assignment or hearing a lecture on why you're wrong. "*I have come to terms with ending my sentences in prepositions because that is how I speak, but now I have to come to terms with leaving my book unfinished at night so I can sleep.*"

Thank you, and yes, ending sentences in prepositions was scary and, therefore, clouding the other topics churning in my subconscious. Unfinished business is too much of the main focus of our subconscious mind these days. That was not the original plan for our human subconscious but with the lower-than-desired ratings on our love meters, that's what we have to deal with now. It seeks to resolve every hint of misaligned language, not only in your thought-flow but in your verbal recordings as well. It wishes to change your memories so that you can find your fascination-factor while you seek resolution in your misaligned behaviors and belief systems. The reason I say it this way is because your mind will jump ship if it sees it cannot resolve something hurriedly. When something bothers you and you look at it again to see no immediate solution, your subconscious mind will note that you are uncomfortable and grab your attention long enough to move it to another scenario where someone else is not as good at it as you are, or it will take you shopping for yet another new purse. Shopping usually works well to distract me now that I have pretty much learned to stop my mind from making everyone else wrong, but my old pattern would have been just that, to light on someone I could judge as not being as good as me at whatever I was feeling insecure about. Now I have to work on the shopping, at least until I learn to manifest purses to the point of saturation. When the invisible faction showed me how easily I hop onto another boat of thought just because a topic makes me uneasy, I was amazed at just how agile my mind can be, now if only the rest of me could follow suit.

Your conscious mind holds your unique blend of beliefs and

memories and aptitudes and perceptions; they all come together to create your personality. Your subconscious mind carries a portion of that personality too but it is alienated from your consciousness in that it remains hidden most of the time. It's that haunting side of you that stays in the basement working morning, noon and night to keep the simmering pots on the back of the stove from boiling over with unfounded whims and wishes and n'er do rights.

That personality factor that lies hidden in the old kitchen in the basement really wants to reunite with your conscious mind. That is part of the veil-thinning you are experiencing now. The consciousness level of the subconscious is dialed down in that you are not privy to every wish and whim you experience. That way you can live your life without another layer of stress heaped on the already over-flowing platter of life.

In metaphysics, love is the divine movement of all energy, meaning it moves naturally towards good/God. Any deviation in that flow will result in a negative motion that can be traced back to a fear of survival, which will at some point include an evolution of reasoning to the point of self-doubt, the source of a whole heck of a lot of our negative e-motion/mind-movement. We experience fear from morning until we go to bed and then we live in fear while our subconscious tries not to fill us with dread while it works on various alternate reality scenarios that will serve to quiet the unresolved mind. That is our dreamscape. Is it any surprise that our subconscious mind might be slightly immature in reasoning ability? We keep it locked up with our fears and then wonder why it plays the moldy oldies for us every time we try to rush our morning routine.

Let's look at mine; all normal stuff but enough to keep my subconscious churning butter all night. My husband just turned 60. He is going to want to retire sometime in the next ten years. I quit my job in 2004. I had peaked and taken a nose dive as far as being needed there. There was an element of shame in not being wanted that was causing my heart some physical problems but I was never diagnosed with heart disease other than hyper-tension.

We made enough to live comfortably but somehow we used my

401K on a car because Ken made enough for both of us. And in 2006 we sold our house for twice what we paid and bought one that cost three times as much. We still owe ten years on that mortgage and the payment is high enough that Ken will need his job to make the payments. Somewhere in that transition, be it smart or stupid, depending on which day we look at it, the bottom fell out of the real estate market. The back-up plan was that we could always sell it if it became a burden and use the equity to buy something smaller. I don't know if that would work anymore. We had just managed to sell at the right moment and one year later real estate took a nose dive in value.

Ken left his job of twenty-seven years because the stress was making him sick too. He passed out one day during a sales presentation. I talked him into quitting and that was no easy task. He had tried periodically to find something less stressful but there wasn't much out there. He was always so type A in work ethic that he had only missed three days of work in twenty-seven years. Rain or shine, sickness and health, childbirth and death – nothing kept him from his appointed duties. Dudley Do-Right had nothing on Ken. But he quit and we lived off my part-time work and a clump of his 401 K. There was plenty of time to rebuild the retirement. Then he found an interim job that he managed to turn into something well-paying and far less stressful so he stayed. The economy was becoming more fragile, however, so the benefits just weren't there. There was no retirement or 401K, and Ken resisted my urges to open a retirement account or just save. He kept waiting for some big chunk of money to fall out of the sky so he could save in big clumps.

Can you see I am getting a little nervous on this one? His job is here to stay, hopefully, there isn't anything out there anymore – and if you're sixty, they don't want you. The health insurance is so high it is pathetic. It was just upped another $50/month, putting us at almost $900/month for health insurance that has a $10K deductible, and another $100/month to cover the health savings account which covers about everything because the insurance doesn't cover anything.

During the height of my fear-flush a few years ago, we both had to visit the emergency room, him in an ambulance and me at least still walking, but barely. The bills totaled $6300. Our trusty and expensive insurance paid 80% of $300 – the rest was our baby. This remark is the snark of a non-love vibration but I feel like we're paying an insurance mafia for non-existent protection.

The new house is perfect for us. We have a special-needs son who is fairly high-functioning and this way he has his own space. It is as though he has his own apartment but we are right here with him. He could not live on his own but now he is much happier and sure of himself. Having his own space was one piece of his happiness puzzle. Plus, I have a nice office for clients.

So here we are, living comfortably on Ken's salary. Brian works a very short day; it mostly serves to make him feel good about himself and as a socialization tool, but it requires that I taxi him back and forth on week-days. By 2:00 PM, I have already driven two hours every day. And driving makes me tired.

"Why?"

I don't know; it always has….

"Because you can't get on with what you need to do – that's your mind speaking, not us. We say you are tired from the stress of working. Not that job, the one you have now. You know where you are but no one else does because they all go to work every day. You are seen as having a life of luxury even by your daughter, who works as hard as you did when you were her age, minus the responsibility of a husband and two kids. She is well. You are well but you are both full of misconceptions about what it takes to raise a child or care for an animal, as is her case, or keep a house on even keel."

"You are not the ones who are tired; your hearts and minds are. Why? Because you are layering your time and your duties on too much."

So they've been telling me and I can see the truth of it when I work on clearing my emotional body of contaminants. But how do I convince my husband of that? He thinks I sit around and watch TV all day. This age-old dilemma isn't going to be solved anytime soon so I will just move on but it is one of the pots simmering on the back of the stove of my subconscious-mind-awaiting-resolution, and let me tell you, that is one industrial sized kitchen back there.

We are comfortable but Ken stresses about retirement. I do too but in different ways. I keep telling him that we are not statistics, but children of God and that if our motivations are more in a love vibration, we will manifest what we need, even if it is a job, and I believe that most of the time. But back there simmering in the crock pot of life is the fear that the house isn't paid for and what if something happens to Ken? Who wants to hire a fat, old lady? I still have half a brain but I just can't sit there chained to a desk for eight hours a day ever again.

I am a psychic and do a good business but that doesn't pay the bills. How type-A do I want to be and where does my intention collapse when going from wanting to be of service to how much money can I make? When my intention falls into fear, which means *when my motivation is more about making money*, my guides are more concerned in giving me lessons to find my way back to a positive outlook than in helping the client or in helping me find more business. Mounting my surfboard and holding my balance on the love-wave can be tricky.

In truth, I know the concepts that come down from on high well enough to do a good reading without their conscious input, but lacking that type-A marketing gene, I won't be making the house payment with my good looks or with psychic readings unless something changes. I really don't like to 'sell' myself. I can sell the house but I could lose every bit of equity and *"enough already."*

Right. Thanks. I am digging a hole that has my subconscious kitchen help calling in the catering service for more help. The pots are overflowing and piling up dirty along the walls of my subconscious. Ain't no pretty back-splash gonna' keep this mess from creeping up on ya'.

And so you see how it goes. Our subconscious doesn't have time to come out and play during the day because our dream state is trying to fix all that's wrought with complications. But like every other oppressed faction out there, my subconscious mind wants liberation and is threatening to come out into the light of day with her voice. 'Seen anybody acting like they lost the filter between their mind and their mouth lately?'

The missing filter syndrome is a sure sign the sensitivity knob is up on high, standard swirly procedure, so that we can see our inappropriate

30

and immature raw emotional reactions in play. They sneak out loudly enough that we can't deny their existence with the layers of subterfuge we use to climb our strategic ladders to the top of our goal-based disciplines. Our survival-based motivations, at least in the United States, have come to include several layers of corporate strategy that instills in us the idea that we never have enough. I once had a boss, sweetheart that he was, who said he never listened to music while driving, and since sales was our game, driving was our middle name. He always made sure he had a few motivational or teaching CDs with him because, as he so innocently put it, music is only bubble gum for the mind. I am here to tell you we all need more bubble gum for our minds so our subconscious can spend a little more time cleaning out the fear that puddles around our perceptive windows.

So the subconscious is really the scrap-booking process of our life. The cherished and not-so-cherished memories that lie hidden in there seek resolution to a love-based format. That's why it is so hard to ditch the behavior patterns we hold now – they are filed erroneously – with our fears. I named my subconscious mind last night. I am calling her Meander because me and her wander through the back woods of my thoughts all night just looking for the underfoot crunchies that I forgot to sweep away. I want to sleep; I really do. And I insist that she allow me just a few minutes of the bliss of unconsciousness before I have to get up, but she doesn't care. She's tired of the night shift and wants a normal life too. She is making me stay up and help with my own mess.

Every time I have to get up with an alarm, the underground buzzer rings in my mind and I slip back in time to when there just wasn't enough time. I swear that starts Meander on her journey. It is like a built in alarm that says 'hey, don't go to sleep because you don't have enough time to even think about it. Get back there and finish those dishes and figure out why Martha gets mad every time you park in her favorite spot.

For a period of about eleven years, I worked with another channeler. She heard her guides consciously and for the most part I heard mine subliminally. We worked amazingly well together and even co-authored a book. When first approached to work in tandem, I was given the incentive to run all my questions by her guides and she would provide the answers.

I had such a fascination for this process that I believed I had been handed a million dollars – tax free. And I loved it. I would ask question after question and she would supply me with long, flowery and detailed answers that were nothing like I got from my subliminal-superconscious. Mine were brief and to the point. It was so much more magical to get the long, winding version.

During that time period, I amassed considerable files on every topic that crossed our minds. I was so amazed by the process that I kept every fleeting thought that the computers recorded. Curiously, that meant everything she wrote because at that time that was how she channeled most information, but I never considered my own information important enough to file. That aside, I spent way too much time with a project that became impossible to manage by trying to file and cross-file every bit of information she produced. I had to make sure every possible scenario was available in every possible folder, just in case Edgar Cayce ever wished to compare notes. I literally buried myself in files that I would never see again because I would never finish filing the new stuff.

I see now that I had become the subconscious mind, frantically filing until I lost sight of my conscious voice. Because our filing system stems from such a well-ingrained, fear-based motivating factor, we have become like hamsters running on the wheel to nowhere trying to clean out our cages of life. During my stint as self-appointed office manager here at Spirits r'Us, I could hear my own guides urge me on to keep those files well and in order but now I am not sure if it was just the analogy for me and my subconscious or if it was so I could explain this concept to you later, but either way, we are still trying to file all the old files under *resolved to love* and the new ones still need purging too. Here enters the fear-flush; angelic intervention in the form of a swirly designed to create a finish-able file system and help Meander find her way back to my conscious awareness. By the way, remember that time **60 Minutes** did a segment on a group of people who could remember every day of their lives? Well, if Meander manages to liberate herself, that's how she rolls. She can point you to the instructions you read three years ago on fixing error # e800c16c**fu** and any other tidbit that is stored in your life recording, not to mention help you find your son's softer side when he is having a meltdown, which indicates a direct line to the soul apparatus of those you love and care for.

Did you ever wonder why it is easier to remember the feelings of a fight or flight situation than it is the emotions of just curling up on the couch with a good book? First off, there is an issue with the feeling intensity. We have become accustomed to sensationalizing our emotions so that we can be heard, seen, felt, or just to remind us we're here. There's just too much going on. We seem to operate out of the intense end of the emotional descriptives to help us focus on the issue in question. There are too many layers of unresolved issues that seem to never get better all because we cling to the same old belief paradigms. Requiring a fight or flight adrenaline-based emotional reaction, even when it is tied to thrill-seeking, indicates an inability to find self amid the chaos of life. A true love vibration is not manic; it does not include intensity in any form. It can best be described as 'being at peace with self and the world around one.'

CHAPTER 3

WORKING UP TO THE SWIRLY

We're in school again. All those dreams of lost locker combinations and missing the bus are reality while we sleep – or while we can't sleep. It's all there, stored in our subconscious lockers of memory, filed with the appropriate fight or flight response that started a whole pattern of fear-based triggers and reactions. The good news is there is divine intervention out there that comes in the form of managing the fear that rests in our subconscious. The ouchy news is it just might keep you awake when you most want to sleep and it will most definitely make you tired.

The year 2012 has been here and gone and we're still here. I am not expecting the end of much except perhaps a reduction in our fear-based emotional reactions and maybe, just maybe, we'll learn to look at prophesy in a more realistic way. One possibility is that the Mayan's left us a prophetic invitation to our own graduation. Our consciousness was supposed to be ready to graduate, complete with PHD and the official ok to climb the ladder of mental awareness beyond what has been considered normal or even possible up to this point. The stuff of legends, if you will. Our minds are the real us. Had we managed to hold our vibration of mass consciousness up in a higher resonance of love, we would all have been graduates of Mugwarts by now, complete with doctorates in the higher arts of love and peace, governing without strategy and healing with just a smile. It is the energy of the fear that has become intertwined in our perceptive windows that holds us muggle-bound.

Once upon a time, way before even a proto-type of us existed, there was a decision made on high by a council that voted to keep watch over our forefathers and to allow the vibration of mass consciousness to fluctuate of its own free will. For a while the natural evolution of our physical world went well, with peaceful beings learning the arts of life and creation from the slower dimensions. But when our minds began to play with the fear more than normal, the love became harder to recognize and it became necessary to call in the higher dimensions again and to make a decision as to just how far this vibration would be allowed to fall before divinity would intercede.

Since then we have woven the tapestries of our lives over and over again, hoping for just the right patterns of awareness to move us beyond our personal best. Progress has been slow-moving but we're coming out with brighter threads of existence and longer-wearing fabrics so the weave of the carpet is stronger than ever, but still we require the additional help of flushing the fear-based belief systems that pill and snag our realities with even the slightest stumble.

As our belief systems expose their holes of wear and tear, we will flounder until we can find our foothold in truth. For me, that meant going back to the basics of metaphysics, to the universal law of the ancients and the new wave thinkers too. For our purpose right now, the most basic truth in metaphysical philosophy is really quite simple; Love unifies and Fear separates. So when I talk about love, I am talking about any motivational force that brings unity between us. When I speak of fear, I am talking about any motion, mental, emotional or physical, any force that fosters a separation between us. As a reminder, motionating force amounts to the combination of your raw emotional reactions combined with your true motivation, even in the case of the most minute random thought. You can apply that measuring stick of truth to any situation in your life and get a good idea of whether you are in a love vibration or not.

"Our own evolution has included a special segment on developing individual awareness. All that means is that we were allowed to separate farther from the Source energy of love than most are when incarnated on other planets. We are allowed more leeway in playing with the fear-based motionating experiences. Through this process, we are able

to develop a more detailed version of life than our planetary neighbors. We hold a key to development that is new and exciting when our life recordings are used to demonstrate what our minds do when allowed to fear. There were those in existence who thought we should not include this chapter of awareness in our books of love but we are the ones who will show what is entailed in this new aspect of being once you graduate back into the arena of love at a more pure consistency than your vibration of mass consciousness holds at this juncture in time."

Our time in this experimental dimension is coming to an end now and the Mayan calendar indicated the agreed upon area of time for its completion. Our research funds are running out, so to speak, and we are about to compile our data and re-write it as a thesis worth remembering. Our graduation ceremony is just around the corner. All we have to do is take a night class or two to finish things in a way that raises the vibration of mass consciousness back to an acceptable and evolve-able level of awareness, back to a vibration high enough that we can tap into our capabilities of manifestation.

"Understanding what the level of mass consciousness entails is simple enough if you adjust your inner frequency to love long enough to hear our words. If that isn't possible, it may be that you're in the throes of a swirly. If that is the case, we ask you to read us again in a week. We repeat, please read again one week from today and see if you can hear what we say."

"That's how the flush works. We work on your inner awareness, primarily through the subconscious patterning that holds the kernel of fear residing there, waiting for an opportunity to show what it knows when a similar feeling comes along. The pattern has an area of expertise, in a way, and once it gets a whiff of a similar motionating force coming through, the gates open and the race is on to connect the dots for you using past performance from a race that was never meant to last."

Ok, so we hang on to our past too much. That is one reason why it is easier to remember a fight or flight situation than just curling up on the sofa with a good book and reading until you want to stop reading. No matter how happy you are, because so much of our lives are spent tied to meeting survival needs, there are too many situations that are emotional downers and every time we encounter one, even though we ignore it and move on to the next task at hand, our subconscious is busy playing the match game with all the old, unresolved scenarios that are similar to the raw emotional reaction you just swallowed. How can you hear yourself with layers of that happening all day? Reading a book, if that is an enjoyment for you, is quieter, but it is peace, and that is the desired end result.

My son fell again today and I heard the crash and managed to by-pass the sinking feeling in my chest and make tracks for the bathroom where I knew he was in the shower. He has some physical problems as well as mental disabilities that really keep us on our toes as to his whereabouts in the throes of his swirlys.

The falls began a couple years ago and at first were not really alarming for me, or so I believed. In truth they were just another pot simmering on the back burner of my stove of unresolved fear. If he fell, he would just get up and everything would be fine. Then one night as I got up to close a window near his room, I must have scared him because he fell out of bed and hit his eye on the corner of a nightstand. The ensuing trip to the hospital showed he would have a black eye but other than that, he would be ok. He did, however, have way too much trouble getting up.

At that point I began to carry a feeling of dread if I had to go near his room when he was asleep. No amount of reasoning with myself seemed to ease my mind. And I began to realize that over the course of the last year there had been several falls and it was getting harder and harder for him to pull himself up again. Then one day later that sum-mer I was out with a friend and came home to find him laying calmly in the back yard. He had been there for probably an hour and a half. He had fallen while mowing the lawn and couldn't get back up. Somehow I had felt this day coming and I was, as usual, cool, calm and collected as I got a sturdy chair and talked him through pulling himself up. The process took quite a while; I almost resorted to calling an ambulance. He is a big guy and at that point I couldn't convince him to just put his weight on me and I would lift him up. And more alarmingly, I had also noticed that his right leg just seemed to drag during these instances.

For reasons I know very well, because by then I was fully aware of the fear flush and how my fears would be magnified until I had no rest but to do everything I could to alleviate the cause of my discomforts, I started the phone calls to the neurologist and the doctors. I was learning to push the envelope when I needed to be heard and I got a chance to use those new vocal muscles time and again throughout this episode. To make a long story short, we moved through all the tests and muddled through the results and even took up weekly stints for physical therapy.

We now have a manageable situation, not ideal because we have weight issues here, but we also have some new skills and understandings in our rescue kit. Mentally, Brian is handling things better than I am; I have the distinct feeling he works hard to show me he is ok so I don't worry. Now how does he know I worry? I keep everything safely locked inside and hold my collected exterior together no matter what – or do I? You know how he knows? I have created a mini-me in him. He has learned to keep things too far inside too. He recognizes my cute little jokes as the masks they truly are because I see him doing the same thing. He may have a lower IQ than the average bear but he is emotionally well-adjusted and secure and appears to have this innate ability to zone in on people and know exactly where they are and he takes his cues accordingly, just like mom.

So today we engineered a plan and made it up out of the bathtub with no causalities. Brian decided to get back to his exercise routine and has been in good spirits all day. Internally I handled things better than times previous. I didn't experience the after effects of shaking and that sinking feeling of dread, but I did go through a bout of sadness that permeated my entire mental/emotional outlook for the rest of the day.

Intuitively I knew the sadness was tied to the fall situation but I was truly relieved to see great progress in how we were able to manage the rescue and how well he had learned to maneuver himself in such circumstances. I suggested he now use the shower in my bathroom, which is a walk-in, and he was finally on-board with that – all no big deal, except for that all-encompassing sad feeling that something was wrong and I couldn't make it better.

I asked and I heard them tell me it would be over soon. They were flushing some of my fear of Brian's falling, and my falling, something I hadn't even considered. Several years before, like twenty years before come to think of it, I had fallen while making a speed stop at Target. The floors were wet and I was in such a hurry that I turned and my kneecap hadn't quite gotten the message yet. The resultant sprain seemed to take forever to heal and I was secretly afraid that extra weight would keep me from ever walking normally again. Such fears are the results of our *war on obesity.*

Finally, up and moving smoothly again, I fell on the ice while in a work-related school in Chicago. The scenario was similar but this time the fear became more exacerbated than before. To make it worse, I was away from home and in a school that was up a couple flights of stairs so I had to walk up there several times a day, not knowing if my knee would hold out or not. It did, I just bruised it good. It healed well, but not my fear of falling; it had become so fight-or-flight based that walking in winter is still, to this day, causing way too much apprehension. The truth of it is this; I have had a couple falls since, nothing traumatic like the first two, and this all in a period of about twenty years. It certainly is not a recurring theme so my fight-or-flight based fear seems illogical to me, unless, of course, you consider that I have been affected by the weight-based hysteria that keeps telling me I am about to die because of the numbers on my bathroom scale. Interestingly, my blood work numbers are better than average for my age group, but that aside, I can't help but be affected by the continuous stream of media-based disapproval regarding my body shape and size.

"My kneecap slides and has always been slightly out of alignment, even when I weighed far less, but the extra weight manages to push it out easier. Your knees are quite healthy and you have no pain, which for a woman your age should be considered a sign of health... The rest is manageable and will repair itself as your mind realigns with the idea that you are healthy and fine in weight and mind."

Yes, they were speaking for me...it happens, too much, actually.

"There is an idea in your mindsets that if you do not weigh a certain number on the charts, you are in poorer health than your counterparts. You are if you believe this to be so and if you are in trouble with

your mental and emotional scenarios. Your belief systems ingrain the ideas and your attitudes reflect such. You were not feeling out of synch until you fell and then your idea that weight was the cause caused some additional feedback to your mind and heart. Your knees are well."

Thank you. So my own falls connected the dots with my son's falling to make the emotional reactions even more intense and misaligned. His situation is more serious than mine, but some of my own fears for both of us stemmed from a residual shame that made it hard for me to face the music with the doctors. For the last couple years, I have been unable to put my fear of his falling aside any time that Brian shovels the drive or cuts the lawn. I move around restlessly, trying to nonchalantly peek out the window and make sure he is still standing.

That all-pervading fear-based emotion is being cleared so I can re-pattern any mishaps that might come up in the future with a more love-based reactionary pattern. I am talking about being able to allow him to do his thing without my hovering because I am afraid *"I won't be able to handle his being hurt."* I am also painfully aware that my ways of swallowing stress have been passed to him and had I done it differently, his weight issue might not be part of the problem.

I knew I could handle this…and I knew that I was living an alternate reality in my subconscious dream state that was causing the sadness and anxiety combination. What this actually means is that this traumatic experience kicked my dream state into the ON position while I was awake so it could begin to clear the trauma before it settled into a permanent position with so many other fears hanging out in my basement of lost emotions and ideas. That is why we are so tired lately, at times our dream state is running while we're still up working; that's what I mean when I say *swirly in process.* Normally our dreams would wait until at least a semi-conscious state before they kicked into high gear, but now they operate as necessary in order to avoid as many sump pump clogs as possible.

I also knew that I would live another dream series that resolved my fears and then I would experience a sense of relief. I'm not there yet because I just relived this scenario for you. It has caused some discomfort in my emotional outlook by awakening the incidents that just played out on my subconscious rewind feature, and by attaching their emotional residue to Brian's new fall in the shower, thereby prolonging my current state of anxiety. It is a residue that wafts in and stays even when there is no conscious reason for the feeling, at least until the dream state reality is able to resolve the fear.

"The mind is being utilized right now as a main support factor in clearing your fears. Your subconscious mind is a wonderful tool for cleaning your emotional scars and reactions as well as your feelings. The subconscious mind devours all that you think, do and say and it rehearses your play in your mind all day until you ask why you are doing it this way."

Alright; let's see if I can make this easier to understand. Our dream state is a facet of our subconscious mind designed to help us resolve our life events, be they simply thoughts or actual mishaps that were due to no cause of our own. When we dream, those unresolved scenes, even the ones from television and the newspaper, realign themselves with thoughts and patterns that seem to match in motionating force, meaning similarities in anything and everything, including emotional reactions.

That is a normal way of clearing your crap while you sleep. Unfortunately, it isn't as effective as it would be if we had a filing system based on more appropriate emotional reactions. We are digging on the concepts of a higher existence but we're unable to apply them to ourselves in any way that addresses our role in regards to our negative feelings about things. My entourage is big on not spending much time filling in the blanks of the past right now because they maintain that we are at a juncture where we need to release the past and create a new reality paradigm based on a higher perspective of possibility. We really need to stop looking at the past as a way of understanding the now because we are not connecting the dots in a clear and consistent manner regarding our own fears and our belief systems. We twist them to say what we want to say and quite often what we want to say stems from our fears regarding self.

So to clear the past without consciously reliving it over and over, our dream states are now being monitored and modified to help flush the fear and to create new filing systems for patterns stored in our life-recording files. The dream state is the primary tool being utilized during the flush. Our higher self is activating certain files based upon events of the past and their emotional residues, and through the resolvability possible during the dream time, it moves us from one side of the pendulum to the other, playing out different possibilities – from what could be worse to what would make it all better, including scenarios where you experience the perceptive windows of the others involved in your unresolved past, and finally, when the pendulum stops swinging out of control and finds a center of balance – you will begin to let it all go.

In the case of Brian's falling, he and I would experience a series of dreams where things would go from the worst case scenario to the best possible outcome, miracles and all. We may also experience the harm that we inflicted on others during these stints until eventually we would have a complete enough understanding of the situation that we could proceed in real life without the fight or flight surge in adrenaline, in fact, ideally we would be going for a reaction based in peace and love, which includes the knowing that all will be well no matter what. That is the process I refer to as the swirly, since it can leave us short on breath and vision.

Imagine a filing system, a giant warehouse of file cabinets from ceiling to floor, where every nuance of your life is filed and cross-filed again and again based on every possible link between the files. Now imagine one giant tidal wave coming in and washing away all the file folders so that all you have left is the material from inside each folder and the empty file cabinets waiting to be refilled. That's the fear flush in a nutshell. All of the negative programming gets washed away and it is up to us to repattern and refile in a more positive way, without slipping back into the old patterns of fear-based reasoning or behavior.

Ideally, our dream state would handle this for us but it is too clogged with negative programming and false feelings of well-being. We don't even know when we're happy. Is it truly normal to want to bungee jump off the Mackinac Bridge or are we just looking for a thrill and because we have come to associate feeling with a fight or flight response, we choose the thrill of danger?

The divine intervention is similar to the process used at the end of life. Have you had any old-timer's moments lately? I actually forgot where I parked my car the other day. The inability to stay focused on the simplest of details is a swirly-in-process sign that should stamp itself on your forehead so you are not held responsible for the accompanying apparent loss of hearing or ability to add and subtract in the checkbook. How many times have you just stared into space and not heard a word even when your husband asked you for the third time 'what's for dinner'? Ok – that one may be more than fear-flush…how about kitchen-duty-flush?

These are all clues you are zoned in on the big screen of the subconscious. Ideally, due to the larger than normal amount of negativity, the dream state would only be used during the night, while you sleep, or even more ideally, and beyond our realm of comprehension, when you take a few waking moments to clean out your mind. At that point, your nights are free to run the dream state as a creative tool – imagine that! But to run it 24/7 as a means of clearing fear is stressful on the physical body, not to mention the conscious mind. Nevertheless, while the flush is in operation, the dream state will run during your waking time too. With all that focus on the underground theatre in play, there may not be enough energy left to catch the pertinent details on NCIS.

This grand, divine intervention amounts to a giant subconscious overhaul where your higher self is more involved in your dream state, making sure your subconscious reasoning gets to the root in releasing the fear and resolving the underlying perceptions that hold your slightly out-of-synch behaviors in check. Higher self is the director and you hold the starring role on the big screen now. You might even play the part of your dear departed aunt Daisy because she may have reinforced your sense of not having anything worthwhile to say. If you think of the dreams as alternate realities, you would be exactly right. They are directed and type-cast by your higher soul energy so that you can finally free yourself from the ties that bind and gag you. If you can experience and understand aunt Daisy's reasons and fears for her easy dismissal of you, you will find part of the puzzle already solved and filed under *resolved to love*.

Because one of the consciousness shifts we are about to encounter includes making our subconscious a more conscious project, we are already experiencing changes in our dream state. Besides the great flush, there is a veil-thinning already happening where we are processing more of the dream state with our conscious awareness. Don't lose me here; remember, all your conscious awareness *is* can be reduced to the way you see yourself and the rest of the world.

Some of you may have noticed that your dreams are becoming more intoxicating than they used to be. Remember when you used to grab that brief flash of night-time awareness and hope you could hang onto it long enough to plant it in your short-term memory bank? Now, because more of our conscious mind is becoming involved, you remember more of the dream state; it loses some of that ethereal quality. You are remembering more and may even be aware of discussing the scenes with another being – a guide of some sort.

Before I get too far ahead of myself, let me explain a couple things. The dream state has not been understood well in that usually the magic you were looking for in your remembered dreams was not the subconscious resolving-activity at all but superconscious communication. That would be the guide rather than the resolution-seeking drama.

The superconscious mind is our connection to our soul and the higher realms. Very often the guidance and the solutions we are asking for will be planted in our subconscious and coded to surface at just the right time, you know, those *a-ha!* moments when the plan finally comes together. That happens through the superconscious where there is this fascinating phenomenon called the Akasha of High Probability. This is where higher self and your conscious awareness, that's you, and anyone else thusly involved in your life, may watch a predicted play-out of what might be coming up the next day. When you experience that sense of déjà-vu or you actually experience a happening you remember from the dream state, you are remembering your visits to the Akasha of high probability. That is another capability of the dream state, but actually that was your superconscious mind in action, and this preview-capability could be a bigger part of our reality if we could clear out some of the dirty pots on the stove of our subconscious mind.

Normally, your memory banks would be cleared of this happening so it could play out in the discovery mode, but from time to time, memory is allowed to waft over into your day-to-day world to alert you that something significant is happening, that somehow you are connected to something divine and protective.

A hundred years ago when I was still in college, I met my husband in a math class. At first there was a tendency to kid around a lot, but as pheromones did their number on me, the attraction took on a stronger, more urgent tone. One night after class he walked me to my car and made his big move there in the parking lot. That night I couldn't sleep well, I kept reliving the intensity of the moment until I finally crafted the perfect scene to go along with it. We were both transient students; we worked during the day and attended night classes, but just as my wishful planning was scripted, my phone rang the next morning and he suggested we both cut work for the day and spend some time together.

Now the question is; did I create that reality with the intensity of my imagination and desire, or had I already seen it on the big screen of high probability and pulled it into my waking awareness slightly before it happened? Let us say, for the sake of explanation, that I had seen the possibility on the big screen and hadn't remembered it as a dream but more of something I had some degree of control in creating. Rather than seeing it as something predestined, these scenarios can more accurately be described as circumstances where we have at least partial ability/responsibility as far as creating the desired outcome.

The superconscious mind had somehow taken the coordinates of my life and looked up ahead and allowed me some conscious memory of what might take place. That's the magic we're looking for in our dreams – but right now our dream state is too clogged in trying to resolve our immature perceptions and emotional reactions. If we're looking for the magic, we're looking in the wrong place. It's the superconscious connection we want, and that is also shifting more to our conscious focus.

When we're finally holding our personal vibration high enough in love, we will find that those hidden aspects of us are more available to our conscious minds. We won't have to sit around and meditate for hours to find our center and attempt a conscious to super-conscious connection, because that's what meditation is all about. It is determining what you want or need and then trying to slow down your mind enough that you can make conscious contact with higher self and get some clarity. You don't always come out of meditation with your clarity either, oftentimes it will pop into your mind later, when you are finally cleaning up the dinner dishes and ready to plop on the couch for a few precious moments.

So what we're looking for in the dream state is that fragment of superconscious connection where higher self leaves us a hint of what is to come or how to handle the present. Because the subconscious is the home of the dream state, our super-conscious, higher self uses that as one avenue to supply us with our clues and sparks of genius.

I was once teaching a class on consciousness and lay down for a brief check in with my mind to find a way to explain how the conscious, subconscious and superconscious minds work together. I get a lot of my solution-based material from the alpha state after I have spent some time in consciously working to clean my symbolic basement kitchen of the dirty pots and pans. This process involves allowing the dream-thoughts to waft into my consciousness and then to allow the solutions to begin to form. I provide some conscious reasoning so as to realign the material with a more positive outlook. There is always a guide helping me reason and sort through the symbolism, even though I rarely know the exact subject I am working with. After a bout of dream resolution, I will begin to fall asleep. At just that point the voice gives me the information I am looking for, provided I am riding the right frequency of love-based harmony (the right wave of resonance) with my request.

In this case, I was suddenly shown a pair of hands holding an ancient looking scroll. The hands unrolled the scroll and I saw a page of ancient writings in a language I could not translate, of course. The voice said, "*this is your superconscious mind communicating with you now, when you are in life and love in the fear.*" I really couldn't translate the writing but recognized it as significant. When they said, 'love in the fear,' I knew that to be saying there is usually a decoding required during superconscious communication because the message must traverse the channels/frequency of fear. It is kind of like trying to hear your favorite song on the AM setting of the radio when the station is an FM channel.

I asked for help in translating the material and the hands appeared again, this time unrolling the scroll just enough for me to see that it had been typed in *Times New Roman* – I remember those exact words being spoken in my mind. Even though the language was now understandable, the scroll closed and disappeared before I could read any of it.

The voice said, "*that was your subconscious mind; we sent the material you need to your subconscious way-station until you have need of it.*" I might have understood it but it was pulled from my conscious awareness too quickly. I knew it was now part of my long term memory bank, my Akashic recording, but the ability to retrieve the material depended on the wave of resonance I rode. When I was on the pre-coded wave of energy, the message would automatically appear as a consciously noticeable thought.

Next, the hands unrolled the scroll a third time and in this instance certain parts of the writings had been typed in Bold and Italics. My eyes jumped to those words but still there wasn't enough time to make sense of the words, yet I had the distinct feeling I would know them when the time was right. This time the voice said, "*We release the material as you need it. It is coded to surface in your conscious mind when your frequency matches that of the words.*"

The visions were helpful for me in explaining the process and in reassuring myself that I am connected to a source of wisdom and knowledge greater than what lives in this head at this moment in time. That inner-knowing does a lot to heal our hearts and minds of insecurity in self. The more self-assured we are, the more aware we are of the working behind the scenes when it comes to superconscious connections.

When I was 14, about 105 years ago, I awakened from a dream that was so intense and so real that it couldn't possibly have been a dream. It had to have been that magic message from the angels to come through with such force. I was walking up the steps of a Roman-looking temple or building. Greek though it may be, I remember tagging it the

Parthenon. As I approached the massive entryway, an old man waited for me. He wore white robes or a toga; I can't remember which. '*We can; it was a robe...*' Ok. He asked me to come with him because he had something he wanted to show me.

We walked down a long hallway of doors, some were open and some closed, until he led me to one particular door. As he opened it, he told me to look ahead. I saw bunk beds from floor to ceiling, full of sleeping people. He said that they had been sleeping a very long time but if I wanted to, I could help awaken them. Then I awakened with a jolt, and the distinct thought that permeated my being was that I was to write a book.

That dream has never left me but the ideas of what it meant have changed over the years. At the time, I was in a world history class and '*loved the imaginary beauty that might have existed in another place at another time because the time I lived then was not so beautiful.*' (a little help from my friends there...) So I made the old man out to be Julius Caesar and the book was to be the story of his awakening to find himself in our current day. The invisible entourage has just informed me that the story was an adaptation of a book already known and buried within my subconscious. "*A Connecticut Yankee in King Arthur's Court.*"

Oh, that's right; makes sense.

Then as I got older I came to believe that I could have written a book based on some of the past life details and confirmations stemming from material given to me by the magic guides who sometimes lie, depending on the maturity of my motivation. Guides that lie would have a lot to do with a superconscious message being distorted by the level of fear in my request. I searched for past lives to find a sense of self-importance, an intention arising out of insecurity with self rather than a group-serving intention based in love. Eventually I realized they were playing along so I could find a false sense of importance, which is actually one of Meander's jobs. My entourage was just helping out by articulating Meander's attempts to help me feel better about me by creating past life scenarios out of tidbits picked up here and there while I amazed myself with synchronistic coincidences.

I suppose that since the mighty fall of the resident wisdom-keeper of the spirits (me), I have learned a lot that could actually be of value in the realms of our conscious awareness and how it is shifting and evolving, so maybe this is the book the dream hinted at. I just finished reading a book that I couldn't put down because it was about a woman doing a little genealogy and found some distinct memories coming through that might have been her in a past life or they may have been a genetic memory, either way, the resulting story and confirming material from historical context were amazing. I have had that sort of thing happen more than once and the stories would be great fictional reads but I have to let go of the need for truth long enough to let them happen. Maybe this book is the truth I need to speak so that I can go back and write a good fictional read without worrying so much about whether it is truth or not. The truth I am talking about is that I was provided with those all-confirming little signs from the mystical realms of spirit that prove beyond a shadow of a doubt that I must be onto some divine piece of the puzzle. The key word here being *shadow*. The divine quest led me to the realization that I was chasing an elusive vision of myself that was far more interesting than the me in the now that couldn't quite handle some of the day-to-day aspects of my own life without feeling slightly hopeless.

In regards to my earlier dream of the visit to the Parthenon, the invisible faction, or my higher self, tells me that they planted the seed within my subconscious in a way that held my attention throughout my life so that I could pursue the dream at any time.

"It was a way of saying we are with you on this, so go and do and be."

So the thing is, during this consciousness shifting and fear-flush process, our dreams are becoming more intense and more intoxicating, more like the superconscious seed planted within my dream when I was fourteen. There is more conscious awareness during the dream because that is one of the goals of clearing the fear, to make the subconscious more accessible to my waking mind. It also confuses us now because things seem to be real and they don't just waft off into the ethers when you awaken, they hang with you longer. Now you have to work to rid

49

yourself of the residual happenings and accompanying emotion. And to add to the confusion, there will be times when you're really not sure if you dreamed something or it really happened.

Over the past several years, I have awakened time and time again to ask what the purpose of a dream was and they would just say '*subterfuge...*' As the veil thins, which refers to the process of bringing our conscious mind more into the processes of superconscious and subconscious awareness, (read that again – it's important) our psychic channels will be used to clear the fear. That means there is a bleed-over process where the alternate realities of the subconscious-dream-state-cleaning-process are permeating the waking mind by wearing superhero costumes that closely resemble messages from on high.

A few years ago in television-land, there was a series called *Awake*. I didn't watch it but it was about a man who sleeps to enter one reality, where he had either lost his wife or his child, and when he awakens, he enters another reality where he lost the other family member. He was at a point where he didn't know which was the dream state and which was his real life. That is an exacerbated rendition of the fear-flush at its highest point of action. The dreams are allowed to infuse your waking moments long enough to confuse you about what really happened, and then when you think you know for sure what is truth, it all fades away. How many times have you wondered, 'did I dream that or did I say it?'

The scene I mentioned in my 105-year-old dream with the bunk beds, that scene showed up in the movie *Inception,* where the dream states were being piled on top of each other to plant a seed of awareness into a possible future-hero.

In *Inception,* Cobb (Leonardo DiCaprio) is a dream engineer who somehow plants a dream sequence into an unsuspecting person in order to plant a seed of awareness that will, over time, blossom to some desired end result. The movie is a good analogy of the fear-flush, with DiCaprio playing the role of higher self. In the movie, he was hired to over-ride the negative programming of a very capitalistically influential corporate mogul over his son. The father had always treated the son as though he weren't good enough. To make a long story short, the dream engineer wove a series of dreams that planted a kernel of awareness within the son's subconscious that would bloom in ways heretofore squelched by the relationship with his father, a relationship that kept him locked in insecurity. He lived an alternate reality or two until he emerged with a sense of having something important to accomplish and with a stronger sense of capability to do so. That movie could have been based on the spirit-based fear-flush operating manual if it weren't so harsh.

At one point in the movie the dream engineer visits a dank and dirty basement full of cots, where a man who reminded me of Morgan Freeman tells him the sleeping people come to be awakened. The scene left me awestruck in that it was the same scene as my dream, with one basic difference – one that is important when you are trying to discern whether your dreams are subconscious clutter or superconscious messaging. The room where my bunk beds lined the walls was bright and sunny and I felt really good about me and the people in the room. It was almost as though the room had no ceiling except for the blue sky. That bright, sunny feeling of hope indicated superconscious communication. In the movie, the dark basement with the all-pervading feeling of hopelessness indicated subconscious activity where fear-resolution was in process. Good to know when you're wondering if your intensely real-feeling dream has a message from on high or if it is just more of your dirty laundry seeking the basement washing machine of your mind.

When a dream wafts through to your conscious mind in such a strong way, it can cause some unpleasant reactions in your normal day-to-day routine and there are times when you can't remember what really happened and what might have been the alternate version of the instant replay button. *"During this period there are things to be aware of and one is that you are listening to us again and not sure what your own truth might be. That did not make sense but we know you are ready to hear it. We are doing things in a way that discourages your listening to us for your fix of higher identity."*

They set me up again….so here goes…

I forgot myself during my time as Rhose – the tail-end of my own dream state. During my stint as illusionary gate-keeper for another channeler, because lord knows she didn't need another gate-keeper, she already had her higher self, something I had yet to learn - I forgot my own validity because I was so fascinated with guide-speak. So in setting myself up for it, they put me through all the magic I wanted just by telling me everything I wanted to hear. As I said, they were playing a Meander-role for me until I pulled my wave of resonance up to a higher motivation.

I had become fascinated with the Merovingian Kings mentioned in **Holy Blood, Holy Grail** and went on a search to find out more about these legendary beings who purportedly were capable of mysterious feats nothing short of miraculous. I really didn't know then that we all had a higher self that was with us every second of our lives or I might not have had to search so hard.

At that time, the internet was there but not one of the staples in our pantry, so all I had been able to find was mention of the wars and battles of the Francs of the dark ages. I wanted more so I asked the guides. At the time, I was funneling all my queries through my friend, the magic oracle. Their answer consisted of a poem filled with information about a Merovingian queen named Ecknoreial.

Searching for Queen Ecknoreial kept me busy for – oh – ten or twelve years, at least until I realized that I was she and she was me and we were symbolically searching for each other. That was pre-fear flush, where they built me up until I was strong enough for the power-washing swirly; a classic bleed-through scenario where my super-hero higher self plays a Meander-role to help me like me better just to ease the simmering pots on my basement stove. You see, in guide-speak, *queen* is just a symbolic way of saying you are learning to master your life circumstances. Ecknoreial is a symbolic way of saying you are of the Eck energy – that's wanting to know and explore the ways purest energy flows – that would be the metaphysical me; always been there and probably not going anywhere else during this lifetime. The Nor indicated north according to my invisible entourage and symbolic north typifies spirit influence, another facet of my being that is just the way I am, as well as reference to the Greek gods and Celtic warriors I was so fascinated with. Why did some of those legendary beings eventually separate and move to the very northern regions of Eurasia? The other hint in the Nor was that I was going north in my upward bound ways of spirit communication. That eee-elle ending had a way of bringing my attention to the Elohim legends and it worked; I was mystified with the Sumerian legends and the possible influence of higher level beings, yes, aliens, if that's how you want to phrase it, in regards to our set-up here on this planet and the vibration of mass consciousness being maybe different from other planets.

Yep, they told me all that, but still I searched for some hint of Ecknoreial in the deep recesses of lost history. They also told me that Ecknoreial was just a title held by certain underground priestess factions who held the truths of the way. I was more interested in the basement window view then, specifically from the feasting-ego-hall, so it worked. At the time, there was a lot of focus on the loss of the divine feminine because the patriarchal way of life on this planet had caused some confusion as to the worth of the female energy, hence the reference to a priestess.

Again, archetypes and symbols at work, but I didn't know any better. You have to watch spirit beings every second, because they tend to speak in symbols that, when taken up a level or two in the skyscraper of perception, will change meaning on you. There was no untruth in that analogy, but there was a lot more involved than divine gender. For instance, patriarchal was symbolic speak for mental energy being valued more than emotional energy – within me. It is also symbolic of action-related energy rather than internal, thought-related energy, which would be classified as female or matriarchal. The reference to an underground priestess faction indicated the subconscious attempts to make sense of life without the proper attention to the motionating factor (emotion/motivation) behind my behaviors, which were beginning to result in a sanctimonious tendency towards saintly delivery – i.e. – 'my Gs said...'

How embarrassing...

But my vision quest continued and I searched and I searched for some hint of an Ecknoreial in European history, even utilizing the lineage charts that stemmed from the Merovingian blood line and then things progressed to where I looked anywhere there might be records of little-known royals that had somehow slipped under the cracks. She was a queen, after all. I was even willing to shell out $85 for some obscure book on ancient queens that turned out to be the same legends you can pull off the net for free. At first I didn't realize that I was Ecknoreial, that Ecknoreial was that superconscious part of my mind that I was trying to connect with. After a while that quest morphed into a search for past life validation. After incessant asking, because here was the one time in my life that I didn't take NO for an answer so easily, after all, no one had ever said *yes* so easily before…they finally told me to look in the years 1327 and 717. Yokaay – nothing like searching for light in the midst of the dark ages. And as an ironic PS, during this search I would tend to look at the clock at night when I was beginning to tire and it was always at 7:17pm. After the search halted I would tend to awaken at 7:17am. As hindsight it all makes perfect symbolic sense now but caught up in my need to find my faux-exalted truth, I indeed missed many such obvious signs because I rode a more self-serving wave of motivational energy.

But search I did until maybe seven or eight years into the search, I had begun to amass a folder called the Search for Ecknoreial, where I documented my pseudo-past life experiences and spontaneous regressions, as I came to call the assorted visions and synchronistic discoveries, and the information passed along per guide speak. I will need to mention there that I still ran every related thought that I had through my channeling friend, Deane, and I must have driven her nuts with all my self-centered questions. I have to thank her for all that work – and yes, the information was a good representation of my higher soul's way of handling me. I wasn't afraid to trust my own intuition but I was more fascinated with the voices of spirit than my own inner voice – which oftentimes did, indeed say, 'this is all bunk, missy; pitch it and move on.'

I couldn't stop looking though, guide-speak mysteries were more fun than working a job where I had lost my feelings of superiority. Eventually I started to peek into that ancestory.com thingie because I wasn't sleeping so well and I found that if you just keep clicking on the green leaves it takes you back farther and farther, even to King Arthur if you hit the right buttons. And heck, if you need to feel like you were part of the original grail quest, there you go! Through several different lines, I found you could just click back to finally reach those kings and queens of *auld* and maybe, just maybe, there might be an Ecknoreial lurking out there someplace.

Well, I'm a little smarter now that I am sleeping a little better and I know that the kings and queens kept their lineages available for purposes that need not concern me, and I even know that we all go back there at some juncture, but still no Ecknoreial. Then guide-speak reminded me that I was searching for a secret title, Ecknoreial was a title, not a name. Well, cool, ok, so I'll just follow these green leaves of genealogy a little more and see what is interesting out there. There was even a point when they told me that it might be misspelled as *Icknoreial*. That alone should have clued me in that my search was slightly smelly, but I was high on finding my missing past when I was more important than I am now and I just couldn't take time to smell those *rhoses*.

With fear-flush subterfuge in play, I bumped upon a name with a vague familiarity who happened to be of the bloodline I started looking into in the beginning – and wonder of wonders, she died in 1327 – sort of. Enter guide-speak: please fill me in with the details of the past. As you may remember, my guides aren't big on details of the past because they want me to move forward and create some new archetypal behaviors and patterns that are based in a more harmonious resonance, but I didn't know that yet. So fill me in they did, with one heck of a story. That's what I mean when I say I had my folder of accomplishments all ready to go so I could take a bow.

Remember that cartoon where Sylvester the cat's son puts a bag on his head and walks away in shame? *"Oh Father…"* that's me now, remembering my swelling head as I found myself there in the trash cans of history. Or so I believed. Again, at least I kept it to myself or the doctor might have written me a prescription for anti-psychotics.

So get this: the name that spoke to me was Isabella de Mar, the first wife of Robert the Bruce. At the time I hadn't even watched Braveheart so I didn't know much of the background but then I found a clip somewhere that said she had been captured by the English and held in an iron cage. When she was finally freed, he was dead and she got thee to the nunnery.

Ok, I did read that, then I couldn't find it again but I did find plenty on Robert the Bruce and his second marriage and the ensuing kids. So what the heck happened to Isabella? Was she the missing Ecknoreial? And according to history, they only had one daughter, Marjorie Stewart. There is a lot of conflicting information out there but in the ancestory.com thingie, there was an entry that says Isabella de Mar had Marjorie and three other kids and that she didn't die until 1327. Of course who knows which Isabella of Mars they were hooking up with? It turns out that the Lords and Ladies of the March were many and I didn't really research all that closely, I just took my first intuitive pull on the slot machine of genealogy and ran with it. After all, my intuition was always right; just ask guide-speak when you're riding that *yes to everything so you feel better about yourself* wave of resonance.

One entry says Robert the Bruce so loved Isabella that after she died he didn't remarry for some time but here she is in another entry saying she was alive long after he married the second wife and she birthed three more babies. What was the truth? So the guide-speak-subterfuge-masters spun me a yarn of Isabella being politically cast aside and then rescued by a friend of her parent's family. And then – confirmation through a magic sign always makes it truth, right? So get this, a friend who knew nothing of this private search of mine showed me an old book that had been in her family for some time. Lo and behold, the ancient book turned out to be about Isabella de Mar's family. It had to be my sign. That's the way it works when you're in the synchronistic flow, but what about when the wave of resonance is too low?

So the magic yarn they gave me was that Isabella was rescued by a friend of her parents' family and hidden away in an underground priestess organization - there's that I-am-searching-for-me-in-the-wrong-way-again symbology – and that some politically active priest didn't want Isabella around because she had some ties to the wrong political factions. In our spirit-based fictional version, Bruce needed a healer and the priestesses sent Isabella and they reunited in secret. They saw each other underground and had three more kids, thus matching the curious entry in ancestory.com. Maybe someday I will pull out that folder and write the story because it was very entertaining, but because at some point I realized that the material was not truth but part of the subterfuge game, I pitched it. It carried the stink of me when I had to be more than I was because I couldn't find the me I wanted to be.

All of that amounted to a subterfuge episode where guide-speak distracted me with a pretend treasure hunt while the fear-flush shoved my head under water over and over to get rid of at least the top layer of ego-based fear that would cause me to want to exist in another time and place rather than be in the moment with the people I love. The story may be bunk but it is just the kind of fiction I like to read. If I can get over feeling like a fool, I might write the story, but first I have to find my center in truth, and that means finding the truth of the journey of *the* soul rather than my personal and not so exalted soul.

You see, one of the reasons I am so disgruntled with the story is because, not realizing that the wave or frequency of fear in my quest would distort the answers from on high, I thought guide speak was flat out lying to me. Now the real truth of Isabella is not known to me and never will be in this lifetime. If I should decide to check it out when I return to spirit, I can, but I am beginning to understand that it would be unimportant to me at that stage of the game. Right now it held my interest with a fascination of how things work **and** - and this is a big **and** – whether it might have been genetic memory or past life memory or even just the kindness of a spirit being willing to look into what I couldn't access from here, really doesn't matter. If my own existence at that time hadn't been clouded in self-doubt and uncertainty, I wouldn't have even cared. The bottom line is this: when we finally flush enough fear, we are interested in the now and the past doesn't matter as much and the future is not a worry, just a possibility with potential for us to shape in our own creative way, which is why we make nightly visits to the Akasha of future possibility.

That's what I mean by the bleed-through that runs through the intuition channels during the flush. We are all becoming more psychic, if that's the way we want to go, but the material coming through may have more to do with your own development through this tricky portion of your incarnated existence than with the magic of your all-seeing eye. For me, one of the big lessons here was that I was somehow feeling a sense of lack within myself to function in the everyday world and so I sought proof of connection to something higher. That is normal at this stage of the game but when I contacted something higher, I began to put my decision making capabilities into the hands of spirit. It kind of reminds me of the Big Bang Theory, where Sheldon tires of making mundane decisions and throws his dungeons and dragons dice to determine whether he should go to the bathroom at the restaurant or wait until he gets home.

It has a lot to do with the mistaken belief that spirit has a plan for me and if I can listen well enough, spirit will tell me what it is. Spirit wants us to take conscious control of our life and move through it knowing we are well-blessed with the capability to carve out our own existence in a way that addresses our wants, needs and desires and holds each of us sacred in our own private identity as well as in being a member of the unifying whole.

We've spent eons searching for the right clues that will show us we are part of something bigger than just us. That's the drawback at this vibratory rate of mass consciousness. This shift is designed to allow us a look into that connection so we can get back to being us – the one with the spare tire around her middle who discovers that her waist measurement isn't even a factor in her physical awareness. Her unique beauty should never have been noticed as having undesirable attributes at all, but rather her distinctive strength of character that holds her steady in a sometimes floundering world of injustice and inequality, where she learns to hold love of all around her as her main motivating factor rather than spending the prerequisite number of hours at the gym trying to redesign her physical vehicle. When bodily size and shape become a focus of importance, we need to know our vibratory rate of mass consciousness has slipped too low, but just what does that mean? My entourage made it very easy for me to understand - and right in the middle of the fear flush – one of those fight or flight moments that I'm not likely to forget.

CHAPTER 4

WHY WE FLUSH, RINSE AND REPEAT

The thing about being in the middle of a swirly is that you don't know why you're there. Fortunately, some of you will go through your swirlys without even knowing it, although since 2012 or slightly before I am seeing a whole lot more clients with amped anxiety requiring a consultation at least on the process, so they know why they're climbing the walls and waiting for the end of the world. The subconscious provides a layer of protection for your thinking mind so that you don't lose the sanity you thought you had. Instead you lay awake and think about something stupid that you said in the first grade and you hope no one remembers your grandiose faux-pas. At least if you're at the point of remembering the past, you know the worst of the swirly is over and you are now being asked to refile all that unresolved gunk under new and happier emoticons.

I was in the thick of one of my power-washing swirlys when I finally understood how the vibration of mass consciousness affected us and what it was. Raising the vibration of mass consciousness is the basic reason for our fear-flush-swirly-syndrome. I had new age analogies up the wazoo to explain it but there was still a thread of me – well, maybe an entire bolt of fabric - that didn't quite get it. Such is the way when you become so ingrained in your escapist beliefs that you fail to see how you might have need of a good perceptual cleansing every now and then. I am talking about those defense mechanisms that we encapsulate ourselves within so that we blind ourselves to the fears that hold us muggle-bound. We twist our belief systems to reinforce that which we ought to change. It would seem that my sense of self had used false comparisons and strategies to build walls around me that were oh-so-magnificently elegant and wise. I could help you with your problems but somehow I couldn't see my own for the forest I created in front of the tree that was me.

There is a pattern to the fear-flush and recognizing it might make certain areas of your life easier. There are parts of it that will not give you a break, but fortunately most of that part is veiled in subconscious awareness that doesn't hit the light of day. When the old patterns are finally resolved, they will drift aimlessly into your mind and then you know it's time to get out the new file folders and start making sense of that warehouse of memories – you know, the ones the tidal wave washed through and left you with only raw material to reorganize. The trick is to refile them with new material, do something new - anything, so you can change that sour-faced emoticon on the files to the happy face. I will try to show you what I mean.

In order to understand this process, I remained awake through a nightmare or two. The process of the swirly will always stay hidden behind recesses of your awareness so that you do not bring additional focus to the very behaviors that require a shift. The reason for that is simple enough, what you resist will persist. To hold your focus on what you want to change only adds to the feelings of uncomfortable progress on your part. We are trying to file our feelings under the happy faces, not the frownie faces in sunglasses.

I have my issues, but some I thought I had worked through. Unfortunately for me, my higher self decided I could sit in on my own swirly-tear-down so that I could understand what folks are going through when they say they can't sleep and their asses are tired and they are sure someone around them is about to die because they can actually watch the dread as it permeates from every pore of their worn-out bodies and minds. The process is painful and disorienting but it is temporary and you do come through it stronger and more sure of yourself than you were.

So the whole of it is that I experienced some of my fear-flush while wide-awake and unable to do a damn thing to get away from it simply because I couldn't figure out how to get up and leave the room without taking my soul guides with me – the very villains that were orchestrating my unpleasantness. I searched high and low for a phone number for the Talamasca but all to no avail. The guides that I proudly touted as my gift turned on me and let me know that I was one sorry-ass disappointment. I felt like a child of the vampire, Lestat – before he decided to become a saint. The effects of all that were intensely uncomfortable but it did clear the need for me to depend on them as my main means of validation. Painful and even cruel it was – and when I die I might even have a few words with the invisible gang about some of the things they put me through *'you already have…'*

"We are not the friends you wanted us to be because you had friends enough in your own world and you were using us to find your belief in self. Your work (psychic readings) *is different; you used us as you would when your intentional line-up was in love and to be of service."*

Ok, true, but the going was rough and I will not walk through the flush again except for a slight rendition so you know what I am talking about. I experienced that karmic thing where I had to live through what I had caused, from all angles, with no way out until the lesson was complete. During one portion of this cruel and unusual punishment, on a cold and snowy afternoon, I sat huddled in the living room, shivering and so chilled I couldn't find warmth with yet another blanket or with turning up the heat even further – the flush gets like that sometimes; you just can't get comfortable. I was at a point where I required some love-based energy to go much further, in fact, to any happenstance observers I would have appeared to be experiencing a nervous breakdown. I was physically too weak to do much other than the absolute necessities and focusing on anything around me was almost impossible since what was happening inside took all my attention. In truth, I knew I was ok but incredibly uncomfortable and wishing for the end of my journey into subconscious psychotherapy. The invisible faction instructed me to get up and turn on the fireplace. That required naught but the flip of a switch so I figured I could handle it but I got up only to get side-tracked and forgot to turn it on. I sat back down and, too distressed to get up again, I hadn't slept in several weeks, a sure sign you're face down in the swirly process, I realized my mistake and thought 'oh, shit.'

My evil, invisible entourage told me they would do it for me and I looked up to see that the fire was now burning of its own volition. I was suddenly amazed and my mind began to scan all the miracles that would be possible if only my entourage would perform them for me. We had already had several discussions where they explained that they do indeed perform our miracles when we need them but if we can do it ourselves, there is no need for such performances, and the truth is, if we had a higher vibration of mass consciousness and were riding individual waves of resonance higher than ones propelled by our fears of not being good enough, we *could* perform them ourselves.

Now how many books have you read or TV shows have you watched where some ambitious little witch just blows on a candle and lights the flame? I was beginning to wonder if maybe I was lacking something because I even had trouble starting a fire when all I had to do was just pull the trigger. I must be missing the fire-starter gene. But let me not be swayed, if the fireplace is on, what else might I do? So I asked if I could start blowing on the candle wick to start the flame.

"Why?"

Of course, *why* – the days of *yes* were now long gone with these guides.

The crux of the answer was that if I wanted to spend most of my life learning to hold a discipline that defied the possibilities of our vibration of mass consciousness, fine, but it would very likely be a waste of a lifetime. What that means is this; the vibration of mass consciousness is a literal magnetic force field of the belief systems, perceptions, raw emotional reactions and motivating energy of the masses. Most don't believe that we can breathe fire to the candle without at least a match, so it isn't possible for the most part. There is a bit more to that, in that our thoughts are not high enough in a love vibration to refrain from doing harm, and should we have that kind of control with something as powerful as fire…well, need I say more? But it is our fears that keep us from believing we can do those things. If we believed we could, and if we were operating with a love-based intention that moved towards the good of the group - we could.

Now that makes me wonder, I can't see how I could ever start a fire using a piece of flint and a stone or stick or whatever the Indians used either. My fear is I would never get it going. Did their belief that it worked make it that much easier for it to happen?

"Yes."

Interesting. Ok, so this vibration of mass consciousness thingie is what keeps us muggle-bound. We don't believe in magic and we don't get magic. But again, it's not quite that simple. The magic comes about when we come from a true an honest intention to be of service – to help others – simply because it is needed. Somehow we have to develop our sense of self well enough that we lose it and become more interested in the needs of those around us. Now don't be confused by that; magic can still be part of our everyday existence. We don't have to be in a life or death situation to be allowed to make magic. What we consider magic is all possible according to universal law, and that works the same in this dimension as it does in spirit; it just works slower so we have a chance to see *how* it works when combined with the stresses of a fear-frequency.

The problem lies in our belief systems that have become tied into our fear-based realities. I teach classes on this stuff and my logo-slogan is *sharing the lessons of spirit guides.* When I am getting ready for a class I sit down at the computer and attempt to outline the material. It never works. They plug in their very perceptive sentences here and there and that causes me to sideline, which works well as long as I am not depending on them to do the whole project for me. But often there will be guide-stemmed statements that bear repeating exactly as they were given to me. My outline often consists of several pages of pro-found guide-speak-statements that by themselves cause one to have to think so much that they lose interest before they find a point of focus. To avoid that reaction, I read the statement, translate the guide-speak and then we discuss; it works well and it includes the magic of guide-speak because we're all still fascinated with the process.

Now as I was saying, energy performs the same here as it does in spirit, only slower. I was going to explain the vibration of mass con-sciousness to a new class when the invisible faction came in with an interesting statement: '*You can no longer eat or breathe without fear.*

Your own belief systems have come to include so much fear-based rationalization as to the whys of your discomforts that we are here to say that you make sciences of our analogies. Put our words away and look at your own life. When we say clean up your waters, we refer to your emotional base. When we say clean up the air you breathe, we want you to look at your thought patterns.'

What they are saying is that they will always speak to us with some degree of symbolism while there is a distortion of fear, which equates to negative thought and feeling. And remember, that symbolism takes on different meanings as you move higher up the elevator of perception. For instance, when still immersed in self-absorption, which is the case when in fear of survival needs going unmet, you might as well, quite literally, vacuum the air and bleach your wells and toilets because you're about to smell every wayward thought you have and you are about to attract and even cause the spontaneous creation of mold and tiny little irritating insects. Thank the heavens we still have our invisible factions to deconstruct our thoughts (air) and raw emotional reactions (water). The good news is that once we rise above that frequency we will learn to catch the pollution while still in the mental and emotional bodies and clear it before it manifests. Imagine, a green world without all the work of going green....

At this vibration of mass consciousness our beliefs are skewed in that we do not understand that we are pure creative force in action with every random thought we have. Now think about that; the last time you were running a little late and had to slow down first for the bicyclist and then the jogger and then the little dog that charged out in front of the car, how many 'oh shits' radiated from the energy wave this is you? I am not saying you were angry at anyone, just having to slow it down in slight frustration. In divine mind, our pure creative energy would have created a few smelly nuggets right there in the car. I, personally, could keep the odor neutralizers in business when I drive – and I am pretty laid back. The point is this: if we could manage our own personal air space as far as holding our minds in a place of peace and love, the pollutions of our planet could be managed with a simple mind-set to refresh and renew.

Relax, you're not in danger of sinking into a muck hole of cussing but that's because of *"our roles as your resident auric-field-secret-buffering-agent."* Yes, thank you. Since at this stage of the game we require some help in understanding our role in creative forces, our higher self plays one role I like to call the *buffer zone*. When they first presented me with this concept I had a quick cartoon-vision of Bugs Bunny's arm stretched way across the sky and catching some whisper of a thought, crunching it up and letting the ashes blow back up into the heavens.

As the buffer zone, we keep higher self pretty busy with our mental constructs of why we sneeze when we do and what happens when we break out in a rash because we changed laundry soap, never once making the connection to what was emotionally irritating us at that point in time. Our lives are so jam-packed with to-do lists and should-have wishes and will-get-to-it once we finish our pledges to the allegiance of following the right-path-disciplines that it is simply not possible to find our way out of the quagmire of stress we kick out of our paths and still take note of all of it too; hence the simmering pots on the back-burner of life again. If they can't be looked at long enough to resolve, they are likely to, at some point, boil over somewhere. My early-teen hay-fever wasn't as much an intense reaction to rag-weed pollen as it was a slight sensitivity to it coupled with the stresses of puberty and parental controls. With no voice in my early teen self-governance, a slight reaction morphed into a very uncomfortable physical reaction. The energy of my frustration had to go somewhere and since there was no safe outlet that included a love-based understanding of where I was, I usually had one whopping upper respiratory infection by the time the season faded. It wouldn't have mattered if I used a green detergent or a bottle of #2 red dye, I was goin' down.

We all know this at some level, but what we don't know is that we are creating the non-desirable scenarios with our overly analytical attention to what we don't want. Case in point: I was learning about the buffering process with the invisible faction one day and I finally reached a place, after running all day, when I was home and ready to stay put. My buffer zone was going to give me five minutes on my own – no energy buffering - just to understand how our thoughts create our reality.

So there I was, that mega-sigh of relief, home at last. Then I realized that I was hungry and really hadn't had time to eat all day - so "Yay! Am I thin yet? 'Doesn't appear so; I seem to be the same ole fireplug in motion; oh well, I am hungry and justifiably so.'

I opened the refrigerator and it was empty. Darn, I wished somebody else would go to the store just once...well, probably not going to happen in this life since I'm here and all I ever hear is 'you don't work, why didn't you do it?' I have to tell you, when I went to work from eight to five every day it was a whole lot more stressful but I also have to tell you that there isn't all that much down time now either. And allow me to point out that there is just a whiff of a 'poor me' attitude in that scenario, which does its number in layering on just a smidge of another fear-based emotional reaction.

But again, we already know all about stress and how to handle it, right? So here's where I was going: I noticed we still had two pieces of cheese, a minor miracle in itself since cheese is the nectar of the gods for my son, and to complicate matters, my daughter, the cheese connoisseur, would be the first to throw the supercilious eyebrow at such unwholesome board of fare, but here I was with two pieces of *processed* cheese. I could make a grilled cheese sandwich; I hadn't done that in forever. Somewhere in the world of low-fat and naughty carbs, grilled cheese went by the wayside. Still, it sounded really good and I didn't feel like cooking; it was easy. Of course my gall-bladder might not want all that fat...I wonder if I have any gall-bladder problems? Oh wow! We have two pieces of bacon; I could go all food-channel and add bacon and tomato. That would really be good....but all that fat.

Well, without my buffer zone to catch my various fears and steer them in the best direction, what to eat wasn't a problem by then; I was so nauseous I couldn't eat. I had begun to manifest my all-that-fat-and-other-assorted-non-love-based-thoughts. That little scenario in manifestation is called the *quickening* by our invisible factions and they are using it all the time just to get us up and ready to get to work in monitoring our words, thoughts and deeds, a must in eliminating the fear-based residue that clings to us at this level of conscious awareness. And next time you experience a bout of unexplained nausea, just consider that your thoughts might have been the culprit. That perceptional shift in realizing where the true causes of your reality originate is called *taking conscious control* and that is also the beginning of activating your own magic.

Before we made eating a sin, we would have sat down to an enjoyable sandwich before we returned to our worries about everything we hadn't resolved yet. But somewhere along the line we added another couple hundred layers of stress worrying about what we eat because our bodies were trying to tell us that we were over-doing it. Over-doing the food, yes, probably, because we were searching for an enjoyment-based option when our day was so laden with insignificant details that mattered but didn't have time to matter, that the motivational energy was beginning to stick, and let's face it, eating could be pleasurable – which equates to love-based - if we weren't sinning by eating the wrong thing again – or in my case, eating anything at all – since I am already fat. Instead of finding the joy in our lives through a relaxing meal, which means finding a love-based operating field, we spend gazillions of dollars and stress points trying to determine which food is still safe to eat and which vitamin is necessary to keep us functioning at optimum health. I'm not there yet, but I'll let you in on a little secret; all we have to do is clean up our thoughts, base them in love, in other words, take our fears out of the equation and find a way to think of ourselves as part of one big manageable whole - and the rest takes care of itself. In divine mind, in a love-based frequency, we can eat whatever we want and our bodies will process it so that we stay in perfection, whatever that may be, for each of us individually. There even comes a point in the ride up the elevator of love that we don't require food at all, only breath. At this vibration, food replenishes the earth part of us, but later, when we're more light in our minds, the air will do the trick. And newsflash! Our body will not worry much about the oxygen percentage either, because our mind and body can work together to create whatever we need for optimum existence. Remember, our goal here is to learn creation, a goal with endless possibilities. But for now that truth is waiting for us on a higher vibration of mass consciousness then the one that stems from fear of missing a nutritional element or ingesting simple carbs for breakfast.

It is our fear-based vibration of mass consciousness that makes us fat. It is our fear-based vibration of mass consciousness that makes us sick. It is our fear-based vibration of mass consciousness that makes us feel like we're less than we are, because we are the divine fabric of god and love all woven together to form one unique tapestry that will eventually intertwine with all the other galactic fabrics to form the cloak of the universe. We are each a magnificent square of the quilt of the universe but we have fallen too far down the skyscraper of motivational force to feel the love that forms the universe. Too many of our true motivations stem from a need to protect self. That's why we're here now, living yet another life of three-dimensional existence, to find our way back up again, and that is why we are losing sleep at night and drowsily dropping off during the day, because we are clearing the fear-based perceptions stored in our subconscious memory banks and symbolic basements. It's time for something better.

At one point higher self explained that once I was able to hold my-self up there in love-based emotional reactions, I would become more self-healing. There is a point on the rise up the skyscraper of motiva-tional behaviors where all the magic kicks in, from manifesting your desires to discovering your own healing ability. We can raise our own personal vibration of consciousness to a point where higher self, as the buffer zone, will do the magic for us until the mass consciousness reaches the same floor of awareness and we're all riding the higher energy-wave surfboard – that 100th monkey thing. Once a higher per-centage of us are riding the higher waves of awareness, the few still struggling will rise up as if by magic because the lower wave of reso-nance simply ceases to exist due to the lack of conscious/creational fo-cus by us. That is how our thoughts and focus create our reality. There are waves of possibility and/or restriction of possibility, depending on the energy playlist you're riding. Should you ever visit the Akasha of Possibility, you would step up a few waves of energy to discover an-other line of reality, one based on a slightly higher vibration of mass consciousness, meaning the focus of the masses is higher in love and the reality has shifted thusly.

An example is in order here…I have asked often for the ability to bring the flame to the wick of a candle with my breath simply because it might prove beneficial to an audience in terms of proof of the existence of our super-conscious self, our soul-family or higher-self-awareness, a.k.a. the invisible entourage. It would also serve as some magical proof that our minds are the key to super-hero powers. Well over thirty years ago, I engaged in an exercise for at least a couple months of faithfully staring daily at the flame of a candle for ten minutes. I learned to hold my thought with the flame until I had merged my consciousness to that of the fire well enough to discern that there was, indeed, some type of spirit within the flame and I could communicate with it. It responded to my thoughts in a way that first danced with my mind and then allowed me to direct it into certain shapes or to blow in specific directions. I knew there was a world of possibility in there but wasn't sure how to make that point with an audience. Now I understand the process well enough and have even tried a few times recently to light that candle us-ing my mind, just like *I/We* did when we turned on the fireplace. When I asked again for that extra additive to wow an audience, the invisible faction showed me how my efforts actually took flight, meaning I did light the candle a few waves up in vibration, but because my personal motivation still held enough fear to need to wow an audience, I was not of a high enough vibration to see the flame, nor was it sufficient in formation to last more than a few seconds. Were I to have managed to light the flame in that capacity for my class, some would have seen it and some would not have been able to but also, those in discomfort of the process would have caused the flame to extinguish almost immedi-ately. As we rise in vibration, not only do we see more as possible, but our motivations are of a more pure purpose, so communication with the elements becomes a very real possibility – but today at my house, I still have to turn on the stove and fix dinner again.

The potential for possibility increases dramatically with every rise on the *stairs of unconditional love for all around you*. If I can hold my vibration up high enough in peace and care for those around me, I can float up a couple more stairs of resonance and simply ask the air around me to warm me or even notice that I no longer feel the chill because the chill is really part of the illusion of fear and once we can spend our lives in ways that aren't primarily concerned with meeting our survival needs, one big hunk of fear, like being cold and/or hungry, will cease to exist. I won't even begin to get into the discomforts of child birth…

I am not the one you will want to come to for help in managing your weight, but I am one you can count on for help with making the mind-body connections. The real issues begin in the arena of the heart, meaning your raw emotional reaction to whatever is happening around you, and your mind, meaning your perception of what is happening when it happens – this is where true creative potential originates. If we weren't still trying to resolve the rupture in the patterns of bonding between co-workers and still noticing the instant replay that includes family members who know how to trip your trigger, you might find one less pill on your night stand, be it a natural product from the health food store because you are now reacting to the prescription medicines, or just the good 'ole blood pressure pills that just got upped to two a day. Either way, your heart, meaning your immediate emotional reactions to things, and your mind, which equates to your beliefs and resulting mental perceptions, are not sufficiently finding their way out of the negative programming. Just because you've managed to sit down and chill with Netflix doesn't mean things are resolved, and frankly, at this stage of the game, there is no way to resolve them without help from the higher-self super-hero action team; hence the fear flush and night school I call the swirly. At some point, we all change our minds and re-align our intentions for the good of the group - and voila! The vibration of mass consciousness rises of its own volition – although our higher-self super-heroes might be ready for a rest by then.

Several years ago my higher self, when acting as a clear and guiding voice of reason, the kind of spirit guide you want but won't always get until we eliminate some of the lower waves of resonance in our outlooks, asked me if I was ready to give up my blood pressure medicine. I said, 'sure, but you can't just stop taking that, once you're on it, you're on it.' The Voice explained that the medicine was no longer needed, that the stresses of working an eight to five plus the rest of my life, especially including my reluctance to go to work anymore, was most of the reason for the medications. Dropping the blood pressure meds was a little scary and I wasn't sure, after all, sometimes they were the evil, invisible entourage that puts you through your biggest fears – which equates to an articulating voice of subconscious reasoning. Was this just another episode of fear-flush while wide awake? You'll need to know this; sometimes in the midst of the flush, you don't always know if you've got both oars in the water. There was a part of me that was as clear-headed as I always am and particularly on guard and another trying to decide if I was being set up to face another of my fear-based defenses head-on. If that means heading to the hospital with a stroke, well then, I am facing my fear of heart trouble – but if you ask me, I can do without that lesson. If that means I am learning to get over the search for spirit as a guiding force, meaning learn to trust the god within, that will only add to my distrust, all valid points – and yet another swirly conundrum. And truthfully, sometimes all it means is you are face to face with another layer of immature subconscious reasoning, another voice to contend with as our minds open doorways to new possibility.

I decided that NO was the safest answer and then listened to calm and reassuring guides explain to me that they have access to our physical bodies as well as our mental and emotional awareness and that they can alter and correct as needed. I had begun to wonder if I might just be a puppet around that point in time, but somewhere, deep inside me, I knew everything they did was for my highest and best good. Now to this day, I am reluctant to pray for the highest and best good because sometimes it hurts, and I knew in this scenario that there was something of significance happening, but still, to say I was overly-cautious was an under-statement. Years earlier they had jokingly said that one of them, and *they* are all our soul family playing whatever roles we require, would always have to play the role of *Our Lady of Illumination* for me – and all of us. That meant that when they wanted us to take note of something, they would somehow illuminate it, whether it be a conversation, a song, a person, or a scrap of paper on the lawn that held a lost phone number. They were assuring me that there was no way I could miss a message or a sign if I needed it. There is never a reason to fear missing their messages, they make sure we see what we need to see or smell what we need to smell if our vibration is dropping again.

In the case of self-healing, I was given several demonstrations as to how they can affect my physical being and adjust as needed, so that I would develop a trust in their ability to realign anything that might go wrong by stopping the medications. They explained that I was over-medicated since I had quit work and moved through some resultant experiences of flush and healing. They implied that my weight was more stubborn with the meds and that I would be far less tired if I let them go. They also explained that normally my blood pressure would be about border-line by medical standards and even a little higher but that I needed the additional surge in blood flow, which means that is my normal, and that my heart and mind were ready to try to reach a higher plateau of consciously managing my internal stresses and awareness.

I finally agreed to stop the meds - gradually. The first thing that I noticed was that my ankles weren't swelling as much and then I began to have more physical energy. For such a long time even walking had felt as though I were making my way across a gelatinous swimming pool, but of course I was fat so what should I expect? The idea of a trek across a parking lot was somewhat intimidating. But slowly I began to realize that I had more energy and the things that stressed me due to lack of physical stamina were receding. Ultimately, I realized that I really felt better emotionally and that my body wanted to move more without the blood pressure meds. I started to walk and even cleaning the house didn't feel like such a chore; it felt good. I had come to understand that my intense emotional reaction to my job, in addition to all the other stresses of life, had caused my heart to begin a shut-down process that was in effort to prolong my ability to live. It had to keep de-sensitizing itself so I could exist in emotional discomfort without knowing it.

At one point, they encouraged me to see the doctors and have them measure my blood pressure so that I could verify that I was ok. It was borderline, which caused the doctor to begin to look into different meds again. So reluctantly I explained that I was no longer using them but since I was also walking, we reached an agreement where I would continue to walk and monitor without the aid of the meds. As a sideline note here – I am **not** encouraging anyone to stop taking their meds nor am I saying that the doctors are wrong – actually I have more faith in them now than I did then but I have learned to be very upfront with them as far as where I am coming from and to listen and make a discernment based on my own internal *knowings*, which equates to me and my guides. Now when dealing with guides, the question will always be 'which aspect am I hearing or which wave of resonance am I riding,' because most of our questions of this nature come from a point of fear. I usually count on a silent inner-knowing since oftentimes their words will first pass along a subconscious area in need of resolution, one that would equate to our random thought processes as we ask a question. In those cases, higher self also provides a subliminal layer of truth or inner knowing so that you can explore your layers of conscious reality while making contact with the higher awareness. There are many different levels of hearing guidance, but there is always an avenue of truth if you listen with your heart and mind when aligned with love. It helps to ask to be lifted higher into a love vibration when seeking an answer.

It occurs to me that readings are much the same as a visit to the doctor. If you come in and say, "I'm here; what can you tell me about me," you may get a lot of confirmational information with a solution-based concept tucked into the package, something to prove to you that there is something beyond our five senses. But if you come in and tell me what it is in your life that causes you to seek clarification, I can get down to business. I was kind of like the first scenario with my doctor. Subtle fears kept me from being up-front with him and just telling it like it was so I made my perfunctory appearance and waited to see what he told me about me. An interactive reading has far better results and so does an interactive check-up with the doctor; something I had yet to learn.

As the fear-flush clears some of the layers of long-term doubts and subsequent behaviors, your own personal vibration of consciousness rises to higher octaves of love/emotional maturity. I can honestly say I am very healthy for my age but I have to monitor my words, thoughts and deeds to keep from slowing my heart sensitivity down. It is hard to hold that vibration at times and as soon as it drops, I can feel it. It requires the ability to lay my butt down on the couch at inopportune times but when the lessons come out into the open, usually the inopportune time was more a lesson in changing my awareness pattern and in forsaking what I was sure I needed at just that moment in order to find the best way to conform to a higher vibration family-wise, a must in moving upward on the wave of higher possibility.

Me alone, I am usually feeling pretty good, as are we all, but me trying to mesh with the attitudes of everyone else in the family, or the world, when I know things are slipping – not so palpitationally comfortable. And the catch here is this: just because the family unit cannot hold a love vibration doesn't have to mean I should drop my frequency. In truth, we're pretty good but family communications can always use some improvements. We all have our own truths, which include our own wants, needs and desires, and if I were truly in a love vibration, their behaviors would be met by me with unconditional love and a true desire to assist, but so far that still takes work because I get irritated more easily now than I used to. That is the result of removing one of those filters I keep talking about. I used to swallow my annoyance in order to keep peace. Now I have been re-wired so that I cannot always hold my frustrations inside. Ideally, I am supposed to address them in a calm and helpful way that doesn't make anyone wrong, nor should I do harm to any being with my own irritated thoughts, however, sometimes, without my filters in place, something far more transparent and immature might just fly right through my mind and out of my mouth. The goal isn't to expose my irritation to the world, only to me, all just part of managing my raw emotional reactions; I then know there is need for self-correction in my feelings/heart.

So for the last eight or nine years I have been clear of blood pressure meds. I was reaching a point in my own vibrational work that I could be pretty comfortable physically, because, believe me, when my thoughts are rolling downhill, my body will let me know. But this family work, where we are working on group behaviors, can be even tougher. At one point I tried taking the blood pressure meds again. For a period of time there were episodes when I would sit down and become aware of a heart-beat in my head. Now I know that can't be good, but my invisible entourage told me it was just part of the rinse and spin cycle. I watched my moods and my thoughts but wasn't finding anything so out of synch – although I am far from perfect – so what's the deal?

They explained that they were helping me to repattern something but I am never sure what it is I am working on when in the early rinse cycle so I had to wait for a spin cycle or two to get the basic idea of my new direction. I do know that blood pressure meds were of no help either; they helped tame the tension but I felt physically over-burdened again; that walking through the swimming pool while trying to keep both feet on solid ground kind of feeling, so I let them go again. They say I could use the medicine but I can also self-heal, but today, at this moment it takes some work to self-heal. There is no magic hand coming out of the ethers to rest upon my head and heal me, to change my physical reactions to things, because – and this is the hard part – I have to change my emotional and mental reactions to initiate the healing. I took my blood pressure reading this morning, it was 126/76. I know in my heart of hearts they ding me with that feeling of a pounding head or heart to get me to shift my focus somehow but the details aren't so easy to grasp in the early stages of repatterning-discomfort. So I know that I am somewhere in a new cycle of shift and until I make enough progress to stay comfortable I might have second thoughts about taking or leaving those old blood pressure pills, but quite honestly, I have found them to be a shoe that no longer fits so I try to relieve the discomforts with my newly activating self-healing app.

I just caught the edge of the news and lo and behold there is yet another new study out that says our sleep habits are becoming more and more disturbed and that all that waking and not sleeping is causing a hardship with our heart-health. *Really??? Ya' think???* That is a confirmation for me that this book is important enough to continue because it is exactly what this chapter is about. We aren't sleeping well because of the alternate-reality-stage of our fear-flush and our bodies are tiring of the stress. Since our heart's performance is heart-tied to this process due to extreme emotional reactions in the dream state, yes, our hearts are fluttering and pounding on the doorways to our minds and we may even require more sleep if we can sneak it in, but after a time our divine intercessors will help us find healing, either with a doctor or with them, whichever works best for us individually. (You may notice that I still have a hard time with those sarcastic thoughts; and that, my friends, is supercilious snark and not a love vibration.)

If you're not sleeping well, it is usually a major sign that you're in the midst of a swirly. If you never sleep well, you are probably having a hard time letting go of the unresolved situations in your life and you are requiring more conscious input into the solution-centered phase of your daily approach to handling things, something like less instant replay and more change in your approach to solving the problem. At the start of my conscious understanding of the fear-flush process, I hadn't slept for weeks and barely had strength enough to drive so I asked my husband to take me to an emergency care clinic. I couldn't breathe. I could barely articulate my words and quite frankly, I knew I had a lot of symptoms of a stroke even though the invisible entourage assured me that it was just them clearing me of my defenses. I wanted to sleep and usually fell asleep very easily but during the grand swirly I couldn't get there. There was too much emotional residue clogging up the fight or flight pump in my heart and mind. Plus, and this is between me and you, they keep us up to break down our normal reasoning patterns, patterns that keep us resistant to change. We all have our unique blend of rationalizations that keep us stuck in our fear-based belief patterns and they are easier to discard if our normal reasoning ability is absent for a time. Sleep deprivation will do that nicely, although, I would think there would be a more humane way.

I am not someone who would normally visit an emergency-type clinic; for me it would be more like just sleep it off and call the doctor in the morning, but this time I was being strongly encouraged by my ornery invisible faction to go. Once I got there they instructed me to watch what happened around me. They were showing me how this night-school-fear-flush was happening to others. As a side note, I had the 'luxury' of being self-employed by that point and could afford to be pulled out of the main stream for a crash swirly session or three, so my grand swirlys were more intensive than some.

We arrived at the clinic and I had to sit because I barely had the strength to stand, so that left my husband to check me in. He has had the luxury of always leaving the detail work up to me so he was somewhat challenged in filling out the oh-so-inconvenient forms that stare you in the face at the worst possible time. He kept asking me questions with answers that to me seemed so obvious that I was fast becoming a snapping shrew. Anger is something I had spent my life swallowing so I wasn't good at it and surely less than graceful. I imagine there were a few people in that waiting room that would have been happy to give me their place in line just to see me gone. That is not my normal way of being but I had no qualms with making total strangers uncomfortable that day.

The funny thing is, I really don't know what my husband told them when he checked me in, but they came out and asked me to lie down in the waiting room because there were no examination rooms available. I didn't want to lay on a cot that would be crammed into a room that was already jammed full of sick people and I had no problem with letting them know that either. So I waited for an available room, all the while hoping I wouldn't faint or throw up. When I finally got one, they took my blood pressure and I remember noting that it was normal, pretty good for someone who had stopped her meds. Then the doctor came in and asked me how I was and before I could even answer he began to direct his conversation to my husband. Now I have a good husband here but he didn't have a clue as to what was going on with me and I was not used to opening up much either. I was instructed to watch what played out. Ken would search for answers to the questions, but in truth, there weren't many. It was like being invisible as I was being examined. So basically, the doctor spent most of the visit talking about his wife and her job and how stressful things had been for them lately. OK. I am not unsympathetic and I know he is implying that I am experiencing an intense bout of stress but I don't believe he said ten words to me and he was so wrapped up in his own stories that they dominated the topic of conversation. When he was finished with an EKG, he wrote out some prescriptions for stress and insomnia and bid us adieu. I really don't even know what he thought was going on with me, if anything.

Alright. So I didn't have a stroke, apparently, which is what I needed to know, even though I could barely articulate my words or remember how to walk down the stairs, but this poor doctor was so worried about his personal situation that he really didn't even see me there. In retrospect, I imagine his wife might have been going through something similar. There are a whole lot more out there experiencing the mega-swirly, in differing variations, and I have to wonder what our medical professionals are thinking when they see these oddities. Does it seem to healthcare professionals as though the whole world is in meltdown or is it just me seeing it that way because my work entails soothing meltdowns?

I won't criticize the care; I realize emergency care is emergency care and that's why I rarely go that route; I never feel as though I am an emergency. So I was in the middle of my swirly, a mega-swirly at that, the doctor was in his working-man swirly and my husband was too and between the three of us, we were probably lucky to get the right name on the paperwork. I learned some things shortly after that time – like exercising that vocal muscle of mine. There is nobody else who can possibly know what is happening with me as much as me so it was high time I learned to open my mouth and speak up instead of getting irritated because no one could effectively read my mind. I had been particularly silent around doctors because I had a fear of my weight being the cause of any malady I might experience, and rather than be judged as being too weak to take the weight off and solve world hunger all by myself, I kept my discomforts under wraps. That had carried on to my son also, but now I am far better at opening my mouth and asking for clarification, even if my time is up because the doctor is fidgeting again. With a $10,000 deductible health insurance policy and monthly premiums getting closer and closer to $1000, I pay plenty for my emergency care and won't hesitate to insist on being heard next time. Again, this is my issue, this not speaking up, not a point of error in the doctor.

These days I am feeling pretty good but for a time I wafted back and forth on taking that blood pressure pill, which at this point was about ¼ the dosage originally prescribed, until I realized that I kept forgetting to take it, period. I finally had a talk with my oh-so-vocal-at-times guides and told them that if I was going to feel this uncomfortable anxiety feeling, this being overly-aware of the beat of my heart – I was going to take the pill, and if I didn't need it, as my buffer zone, please counteract the effects. So I made my grand decision to continue the blood pressure meds and then darn if I didn't completely forget to take them. Now totally discarded as part of my daily regimen, I can say I feel a lot better with them gone, but the transition it took to finally forget about my blood pressure included changing my inner-channel from AM to FM – that meant riding a wave a couple stairs higher than metaphorically walking on eggshells every time I wanted to eat or faced my desires head-on and feared that they were un-meetable.

The invisible entourage is behind my forgetting about my blood pressure pills; they knew I really didn't need them any longer. They alter my subconscious recall; especially during the flush. Case in point, my built-in alarm clock, it's that knowing you want to get up at 6:30 and you always wake up at 6:28, just before the alarm. Your desire to awaken at the certain time is stored in that subconscious memory bank and Meander alerts you at just the right moment. I have depended on that 'mental note system' since grade school but darn if that swirly process didn't wash away my ability to recall my mental notes at exactly the wrong time. I think I even missed an appointment or two during this process. Normally I wouldn't even keep a calendar; I could keep everything filed in my head. So just to let you know, if you're normal mental abilities seem to be slipping, you're probably in the midst of a swirly and you might need to resort to the antics of mere mortals to keep track of things, but it all comes back once you move through a cycle of experiencing the new to repattern the old. Insert your supercilious eyebrow again, but it's the truth.

The thing is, our heart was actually meant to be used as the divine measuring device that would help us take note of the wave of emotions that propelled us – whether our movement was going forward or backward being the point. More simply put, it would let us know when we were slipping out of love. The anxiety that I feel during the swirly cycle is one I don't handle well. Over twenty years ago, on yet another failure-excursion with my weight, I took a diet product that contained ephedra and I had a reaction that caused me some long-term fears in regards to heart health. Add that to the heart-health scare tactics used by our incredibly well-advertised pharmaceutical companies and you begin to get my drift when I say I prefer to take well-modulated breaths with no hint of discord. If my breathing is the least bit labored, I become fearful. This transition to self-healing is at times uncomfortable because I feel as though I am hyper-aware of every nuance of discomfort, and even though I know that such nuances signal a need for repositioning within my mental/emotional focus, I still have fear-based reactions and belief systems to contend with.

So what does it mean to let your heart lead the way? We are always hearing about coming from the heart or letting the heart guide the way but just what is that saying? With emotional systems still wavering in immaturity due to the clogging of our illusionary beliefs and our oppressive vibration of mass consciousness, we can't depend on our emotional reactions to point to the highest truth in a clear and consistent manner. But once upon a time, when we were young in the development of the human species, before we played too long in the fear, our hearts were operating at a much higher frequency and they were not only the organ that pumped life force into our physical bodies but they were designed to alert us to the dropping out of our life force when our words, thoughts or deeds were becoming tainted.

When monitoring word, thought and deed, which is a requirement in holding a love base that is high enough to make conscious connection with your superconscious guidance, high enough to even begin to discover that illusive concept called unconditional love, you will find that your heart takes on a new level of instruction in that is lets you know when you're out of alignment without actually taking on the maladies of the all-telling symptoms. The divine idea is that once you feel a discomfort there, you would close up shop and take a nap while you realign your unresolved subconscious and seek your higher-self-connection for clarity or solution-based thinking. That's the perfect world we're aiming for with the flush process.

My heart and the rest of me are exploring this concept of self-healing and I can honestly tell you that I feel better than I have in twenty-some years, but self-healing involves self-monitoring of word, thought and deed as well as intentional alignment with the good of the group. To let your heart lead the way, you will have to have its sensitivity knob turned back up to a higher operating potential – like it was before the vibration of mass consciousness took a dip. That means you might have to get to know yourself a little better, maybe even better than you have ever known yourself before, and that means you may want to turn on your internal radio and listen to the songs that play in your heart and mind before you decide to whine next time. I am not very disciplined when it comes to diet but I have become disciplined when it comes to monitoring my thoughts, and it does pay off in terms of making life easier. And by the way, if you're rehashing your life's mincedents, whether in your mind or with your mouth, and using a negative adverb – you are whining. Instead of thinking *I don't wanna' have to work this hard*, say *I would really like this to be easier.* That thought will travel up the line of possibility much quicker and easier, and with far less heart-based discomfort.

Since that love vibration thing can be so subjective and difficult to classify, based on the multitude of emotional reactions we have happening every second of every day, monitoring word, thought, deed and intention is the clearest way to begin to recognize where you are in terms of the unfolding of heart energy, of reaching the elusive vibration of love. The process I am talking about is one long touted by metaphysical gurus. For me personally, I have come to kind of feel like my own twin at times, with one side of me experiencing life and the other side monitoring and measuring my experiencing.

The symbolism of the twin as presented by spirit is one that might cause you some confusion. If you are a watcher of signs, the symbology will pop out at you in one form or another. Whether your sources are tarot, astrology, nature, or the study of symbology with Robert Langdon, you will probably notice the reference to twins even if you haven't noticed the upsurge in twin births. I don't know if there is an actual increase in twin births or if it is just the result of the media filling us with every fascination factor possible but the concept of twinning in regards to messages from the divine is often mistakenly assumed to mean the reuniting of two perfectly matched individuals created from the same soul and separated at birth in this dimension – the twin flames. The idea is that if you should meet you will fall into a swoon of love so intense that you never have to experience the normal growth patterns of the average relationship. As guide-speak would say, *that is true not*, meaning at least some of the concept is off-base. Part of the error in that perception is the romantic notion that the twin flame is another incarnated being that is actually the other half of your very own soul.

The possibility of this happening at all is very rare to nil. According to the invisible entourage, it is very easy for a soul to do more than one incarnation at a time and most of them would love the opportunity but the membership in the *"vehicles-available-for-the-incarnating-club has been oversold due to the misaligned beliefs that we would be clear of our karmic residue by this juncture in time."*

Good to know. The thing about a set-up such as simultaneous incarnations would be that higher self would use entirely different sets of aspects to create the two incarnated seeds for personality. Higher self would want to maximize the learning-awareness potential in order to cover as much ground as possible and in most cases there would be no need to duplicate efforts with similar aspects in order to create a recognition, which would amount to attraction, between two people. The reason higher soul uses the symbolic twinning with us is to alert us to the idea that we are aligning with our higher self, with at least some of the consciousness possibility of our soul. Higher self is our twin, our true 11:11. My higher self is me when unencumbered by the fearsome restraints I hold myself within while studying the potential to hold a love vibration when the going is more difficult than in other dimensional realms. I am my twin when I can observe my words, thoughts, deeds, desires and intentions from a higher plane of perception, when I can meet with higher self-aspects and discuss these situations without clouding from the unfinished business of the basement. It is like me playing the role of the smelly Rhose and monitoring the whole process from a higher plane of perspective while carrying a bottle of fu#%-breeze as I tweak my ever-sassy mind.

The flush of the fear helps to alleviate that cloud of angst that restricts our vision until we are able to monitor our own behaviors with some degree of clarity. We are clearing things up now and as we move through this transition; we will quite naturally play the role of observer along with our higher self. That is part of what is meant by the thinning of the veil. Monitoring word, thought and deed to devise a plan of manifestation for our lives, *while still here,* is the next step in conscious awareness. Symbolically, that is when we encounter the first layer of our *double*; when we begin to *'observe and manage'* the cause and effect of our lives.

Coming from the heart is a process that refines itself as we begin to monitor our mental workings within. They are the constructs of our physical awareness and they will be instrumental in creating our vision of the physical realm. Coming from the heart indicates your most natural emotional reaction to whatever crosses your path, or creeps up alongside you. There is a side of this that is misunderstood, and that is, when you are in synch with one thing in your universe, that automatically makes you in synch with everything else in the universe. The truth is there are many facets of emotional reaction happening with us at any second of any day. The simplest sideline on your path may cause a glitch in your emotional wave that only exists for a second or two, but the idea that it caused a glitch in the first place is a clue that there are unresolved past-glitches and more importantly, a glitch somewhere in your present-day perceptions that could use some realignment. That means it is keeping you from finding a true vibration of love. If we were able to hold a resonance of unconditional love all the time, we might not be past our reasons to exist in this dimension, but we would definitely be at a point of higher awareness where we could exist in peace and comfort without the misconception that our purpose for being here is to find the right career or love interest.

So the way of the heart has to do with holding our raw and instantaneous emotional reactions to things in a love-based frequency. That has a lot to do with determining our octave of resonance. However, it turns out that the wave of resonance we ride is a lot more complex than just a simple emotional reaction. It is more like a group reaction to a whole bunch of stimuli that are happening and have been happening and are still happening because we haven't found our solution-based thought wave yet. Once we climb high enough in love-based octaves of awareness, we are able to tap into the wave of remedies and solutions and adjust to our heart's content. It may sound as though we'll never get there, but with the fear flush and in monitoring our thoughts, there is an immediately discernible change in life's manageability.

As our heart meters are slowly being turned up in detecting the love-fallout, we are experiencing some temporary maladies that result from the stresses of being true to the outdated and fear-seasoned paradigms that held us disciplined and feeling above reproach. The flushing of the fear causes many of our most basic day-to-day structures to begin the crumble towards obsolescence and as that happens, our fear of not holding up our end of the agreement takes a toll on our inward processing of self and our daily routines.

To live in the moment, here in the present without the instant replay button of the past kicking in or without the fears of tomorrow encroaching on our now, is one true measure of living in a love vibration. This is proving hard in a new way now that the fear-flush is in play. One thing that is being flushed with all of us is the need to seek external approval in order to feel good about self. This manifests in forms of competitive behaviors and extreme formats of driving self to achieve for the sake of top-of-the-hill occupation, which is easy to fall into if you happen to live in a country propelled by capitalism. I am not saying capitalism is wrong but it has lost its ability to find a reasonable level of operation. The need to expand further and further, all the while crushing our opponent, as it has come to be defined in some marketing venues, creates an unsafe environment for all of us.

If you require external approval as a means of self-support, and we all do at this stage of the game, rest assured you are going to feel slightly alone and out of synch while you learn to reach for the highest internal motivation and self-measuring stick you can find. This means that after a few flushes, you may not find your usual goals worth pursuance any longer. As example, let's take an imaginary marketing manager who was hired because of her ability to rouse her staff to 'stellar performance levels.' After a few cycles of fear flush, this high-energy, goal-oriented lady begins to settle inside because she begins to become hyper-aware of the angst that wells up every time she pushes to exceed rather than to complete at a reasonable level of performance. A few rough bouts of anxiety where the newly-prescribed medication doesn't help will cause her to slow it until she begins to find her new comfort level. The need to prove herself as master of her domain tends to recede and take second seat to a need to find peace within. Taking the fear out of the need to prove self *able* will thwart the mindset of a competitive drive so that the once-driven marketing manager may suddenly begin to call-off as often as her employees, finally accepting rest as a prerequisite for optimum health. The fear has receded in that the need to fight for the top is gone and now the marketing manager is seeking the alone time to regroup and repattern with a mindset that is still somewhat in the blind and most assuredly unchartered territory. Usually she will see me at about that time, wondering what job she should pursue because she has lost her drive in the one she has. I might add here that all psychics are different and carry different areas of specialization. I am better known for a more therapeutic, problem-solving-type consultation than for providing messages from those that have crossed over.

The truth is, our fictitious marketing manager is reprogramming her mind for a better job using the one she already has, one that allows her more of a love-based wave of resonance in her performance. Her worries of proving herself have eased off and she is ready to face her job without the confines of fear-based hysteria designed to feed the corporate mentality of win-win. Winning is no longer an issue, just doing the best job possible and with the highest level of integrity possible, all the while allowing for everyone to make a fair profit and to be considered a viable member of a group of healthy-minded working family members.

This reprogramming isn't as easy as I just made it sound. It comes ripe with new fears, fears like losing your job because you're not as driven or losing your status as the cream of the crop. Perhaps we will come to realize that the tactics we use to hold that top spot shut others out in an unfair way. This shift is more slightly unchartered territory because we may not realize it is becoming our new mindset. All we know is that we feel sick somehow when we push ourselves towards our outmoded and fear-based work attitudes. We are not bad people, we are and always will be basically good with small percentages of misalignment. We are simply reacting to a fear of not being able to provide the basic survival necessities for ourselves and our families while using the same motivational design as previously.

If you have awakened suddenly anytime during the night in the past few years, and seemingly in a repeated fashion, almost as though someone jolts you awake with a certain amount of discomfort, this little tactic is designed to reinforce an aversion to an old pattern in the subconscious-alternate-reality-state. During the dream state, you were trying to slip into an old mindset after the fear that held you there had been cleared, and the jerking awake served to reinforce your subconscious reasoning in that you would not return to that mindset without some physical discomfort; leg cramps and other assorted physical discomforts play the same role. If you're feeling unwell and unmotivated, you may be trying to apply your newly washed feelings and perceptions to an outdated mode of work while the fear of losing your financial livelihood is a very serious matter and not the easiest place to take blind chances. All this causes some internal pressures that will most certainly cause at least a visit to the chiropractor every once in a while, as you assess your ability to hold up your end of the financial bargain with those in your protective custody.

One of the temporary conditions I am noticing on the upswing right now, and I say temporary for a reason, as it is considered to be chronic by our health-care systems but not with our invisible factions, is diabetes. I see the dramatic increase in weight and hear the town criers every night on the news steering us from the foods that are causing the epidemic, but understanding that we crave certain foods because of certain emotional blockages and also that diabetes is considered to stem from missing the sweetness of life, I asked guide-speak for the real cause and the real solution in mindset to offset this dramatic increase in "*insulin obsession.*"

"*Missing the sweetness of life is often thought of as sadness but to us up here it is considered to be a temporary situation brought on by the belief that one is missing out on something.*"

During the change in our fictitious marketing manager's motivation, I can certainly see a conundrum in that no matter which direction she might place her focus, she may feel as though she is missing out on something important for at least a period of time. I can't pretend I know all the answers but I do see a trend towards our hypothetical scenario in that in unknowingly changing her motivation from a competitive mindset, the resultant feeling of having lost her comfort zone can surely cause a rift in finding solid ground to regroup and revive herself. Our fictitious marketing manager might think she is exhibiting a lack of caring in her job or her gym workout and fear the possible consequent failure or loss. What has happened is the motivating force, the drive that pushed her forward, has changed and left her feeling like a non-performer, even though her work performance really hasn't changed at all. All that is changing is her inner motivational force. No one else even knows anything is happening except that she might seem slightly more distracted or out of sorts. Her feeling of letting self and self-discipline down causes a race to find her old pattern of motivation, but every time she returns to her old motivational mold, she will experience some sort of physical discomfort that will keep her seeking comfort in a different way. At this point, Ms. Marketing Manager may experience a craving in sweets, alcohol or even a little snort of the slow-smoke, whatever might ease the physical discomforts that arise as a result of her missing gumption-gene.

The good thing about these episodes, which will be scattered along your life's journey for the rest of this lifetime, is that they tend to heal in and of themselves once you find your comfort zone in a repatterned existence of motivating self with an emotional wave just a few degrees higher in our cause of being *for the good of the whole*. Once we complete the swirly cycle that removes the kernel of fear from our perceptual behavior, and once we replace our motivation with something more in line with the good of the group, our body will react with a good dose of self-healing hormones. That doesn't mean that you shouldn't visit the doctor and follow the directives that feel right for you, but once the healing is in place, your higher self will either subvert the side effects of the meds or you will find yourself asking for further testing and requesting a trial period without them. You will see far more of this self-healing phenomenon in the next several years.

Guide-speak tells me that swirlys are now a way of life, as are the stops and starts of forward movement as we learn to repattern our perceptions of self and the world around us. *"There are instances where the clearing of the perceptual wonders we find in the midst of your mind can take place while you undergo a brief respite care procedure."*

They are saying that if you're in a circumstance that allows you a break from your normal day-to-day routine, such as a medical procedure or recovery time after an accidental mishap – they are using the break to amp up the swirly sessions, so please be aware that healing may some take additional time.

"After a certain amount of progress is made, we allow you some recourse in that you can tell us when to give you a break and when to proceed. All in all, we are moving through this with each one of you in a way that alleviates your mind of the fear-based ties that bound you to your old ways of being and life-long attitudes."

CHAPTER 5

THROW AWAY YOUR DREAM JOURNALS

I keep talking about the **dream state** as though it is purely to hold the files of our lives as we work to organize them in a more love-based reality. The truth is there is a lot more potential in there than we realize. We can use the dream state, that raw, creative energy that exists in a quarantined state, as a rehearsal for creating our own realities. This goes while we sleep and in the day, such as when we daydream, but we are not really clued in as to how best to access this or how to perfect our creation techniques. I want to write a new chapter for this book but first I have to resolve the rebellious and revengeful behavior my son is throwing around, otherwise my dream state is busy trying to resolve it for me and I can't quite wade through it effectively enough to access the drawing board for my session in writing design. Does mothering never stop? I want to ignore it and write but I know I have to address it or it *"simmers back there on something higher than LOW, so it keeps me from finding out what I want to know."*

The dream state is, indeed, a complex and fascinating area of study when you consider that, at least for now, we are only allowed a small portion of the whole. The top layer of the dream state is Meander and her job is cleaning the energy in our Akashic record for this life, our long term memory bank, to a high enough frequency of peace and harmony with all, that it can be cleared of karmic residue. That sleeping part of us that lives down in the dream state working to elevate our understandings to a point of clarified love is really working overtime. As spirit beings we bring with us an agreement with the universe to clear and clean the energy we use while exploring the possibility of the dream state – and here's the sticky wicket – our lives are part of the dream state energy. The physical dimension exists in something called the *world of form,* and the *world of form* is an actual part of the dream state of our creators. It is one of the dream states of the higher realms. In return for our use of its energy, it is up to us to clean said energy and send it back to the universe with a high enough vibration that it can be used again as a creative tool. The time delay that we are allowed for its cleaning is called karma.

The swirly is an amped up cleaning process where soul guidance becomes more involved in the alternate realities as well as in breaking down old defense mechanisms and behavior patterns long held as healthy reality. In truth, we design our lives around our defenses, our fears of not having enough, of not being good enough, of not feeling connected to those around us on a deep enough level to feel wanted, heard and loved. It's not our fault that we see it that way; we have spent eons in survival mode without the ability to create our wants, needs and desires – the whole purpose of existing in the dream state to begin with. We came here to design and build whole universes but because of the dirty residue of a few mistakes made long before our existence, we seem to spend our lives on a creation journey of finding ways to make life easier; to survive in our physical circumstances, whether that means paying bills or designing new plans to maintain our opaque perceptions of perfection. The windows to our desires are clouded with the fears of not having our life circumstances met without work and hardship. We really need that law of attraction to kick into ON, and for that to happen we will have to endure several mini-series' of ourselves in the alternate reality dream state living out the worst that can happen, how our actions affect others, how their actions have affected us, and finally how we can all come together as one big happy family. Is it any wonder that anxiety levels are up? This cleansing is a new part of our responsibility in moving upwards in evolution. We have learned as much as we can in living purely from a physical perception; it is time to incorporate the lessons of the higher laws into our day to day existence so we can skip making a living and start living like the maker of our circumstances. Our motivations are mostly the result of, since the dream state is back-logged with unresolved energy, our attempts to find peace with what has already happened. This keeps us from understanding self in terms of now.

The dreams that take place during the swirly are layered a little deeper so that you do not have recall of the happenings. They are more emotionally painful since Meander doesn't always veil off the reality of the situation in symbology. That's how she works in her normal mode; using symbolic scenarios to help you resolve the deeper hiccups of life so that your emotional field, which will ultimately become the seat of your motivations, does not cloud in further fear and discomfort. In the swirly, your entourage will hold you captive in an alternate reality where you have no choice but to endure your fears from every possible angle. That means you may become the religious fanatic you find so hard to tolerate, at least until you see why said fanatic finally found his or her voice in touting a dogma that to you may seem illogical and even harmful. Once we learn to look a little deeper at why someone does what they do, our understanding of their behavior makes them more likable, more like us. We are then one step closer to riding that wave of love for the whole. Our needy sense of self wants us to stay in a limited pattern of making sure we are well and cared for no matter the circumstances. But in the higher love vibration, where we finally realize that anything and everything is manageable, our goal at this stage of the game should be to get everyone else up and self-assured that all is well so we can move on to bigger and greater endeavors than finding the right career, which equals work, which equals going right back to where we started.

Unfortunately, until we learn to become less self-obsessed, meaning until we learn to recognize that we have what we need and what we want is something different than what our marketing experts tell us, the idea of wanting to go beyond what has been thus far accomplished is beyond our normal realm of comprehension. We still have far too much energy invested in proving self as special, which when taken a layer deeper means the discovery of self-worth not as a gifted aspect but as a point of identity – I AM therefore I am good enough. As a unified whole, we have capabilities far beyond the reach of what is considered normal, if we can move beyond what we lazily consider to be human nature.

During my major swirlys, when my entourage would diagram every random thought I had, I would feel an urge to explain the whys of my less than perfect logic. Every time I would reach a point of saying, *it's human nature, or I'm jealous,* the kinds of summation that usually cause our audience to nod their heads in agreement and move on to the next topic, they would stop me and insist I go a layer deeper as to the whys of what I accept as normal – because negative emotional reactions of any kind are not normal and should be trained to climb to a higher wave of maturity. That is what is happening during our swirly sessions. We are climbing over these childish emotional reactions until we have enough understanding to move our immature reasoning up a stair or two on the pathway to self-actualized maturity. Once the understanding reaches a point of completion in the alternate reality dream state, your entourage will hit the light of day with you in repatterning the old outlooks and defenses that resulted from said immature emotional reactions. The process takes a while and there are layers upon layers of clean-up necessary but slowly we are achieving a higher sense of what is normal and acceptable in regards to human nature.

I have clients that are identical twins and both are quite gifted artistically. They are very similarly inclined to my wavelength; meaning both are more liberal in political views and a little shy of wanting a religious handbook to point them in the right direction. Religious views aside, both are really happy about the progressive viewpoints of the new pope and are doing some artwork geared to show support for his philosophies. One sister, Kathy, will be exhibiting her pope tiles at an art show where he will be visiting, and the other twin, Patty, wanted to include her artwork as well. She was strongly impressed to paint images of animals getting along peacefully in new and unexpected ways. Patty had a consultation with the guides for other things but when they planted the words *pack* and *mentality* in one of her answers, I felt the pull to string the words together and see what happened. I was doing my stint as translator of the guide speak when I realized that transcending the pack mentality was some of what she was trying to depict. Pack mentality, survival of the fittest, these things that we see as normal with our animals and therefore judge to be normal for us, are not only abnormal for our animals but are clearly bullyish on our part. As we train our childish emotional reactions to rise above that of self-protection, our animals and even plant life will further develop to becoming at peace with and as one with us communicatively. When my animal-artist friend saw the value in what she wanted to do, she had chills running up and down her arms, her confirmation she was on the right path. At that point the guides told her once she finished some of the images, she could look at the background and she would see the face of St. Francis, patron saint of the animals. Her guides would provide the magic – and all because her new love frequency allowed her to see the beauty of another perceptive window; one that differed from hers but still held value for many. In a nutshell, we can employ whatever philosophy we want, but we will get to the same spot on the love barometer even while using such varying and unusual pathways.

So that's where we're going and how we're getting there depends a lot on what happens during that swirly dream state. Now that our conscious mind is more awake during the dream process, it brings back a lot of intense subterfuge. We may awaken with a sense of pervading gloom and snatches of memory that make us feel creepy about ourselves and some of those around us. This residual creepiness needs to be cleansed by our conscious mind and moved to higher ground, to be recognized as the cleansing it is rather than guidance or prophesy for our day-to-day existence. There is an irony here in that as we become more conscious of our dreams, we should also be aware that said dreams are byproducts of a cleansing of our own gunk in a way that makes them less than reliable in terms of superconscious messages and higher realm reasoning. If your dreams are speaking to you loud and clear right now, keep in mind that your good, solid reasoning should be employed in making final decisions. Don't base your plan of action on the dreams that came through so loud and clear that it must be St. Honesty telling you which direction to take in severing ties with your dissident child. True higher realm messages will never make one person wrong or take sides in a conflict. More likely, a higher realm message would be a discourse on seeing things from a higher perspective and releasing your hold on being right to allow a healing of both parties to take place.

Last night, while dreaming, I listened to guide-speak explain some of the symbology they are using in my current dreams in regards to both the clearing of my fear and in areas of my development-plan for forward movement at present. They said the number six would show up as a sign to focus on community service, where my motivating force is now being watched more in terms of my desire base and how much of that includes the welfare of more than just me. I clearly remember them telling me to 'think of it this way...' and then I saw myself put something into a gift box which was neatly lined with white tissue paper and an elegant white sticker. The gift made me think of white gloves. I was being put on notice to consider giving more of myself in terms of helping others. I *knew,* rather than was told, to consider taking dinner to the in-laws as part of my normal routine. I remember seeing flashes of other situations where my focus would begin to shift to that of my kids or husband or brother, rather than *what else might I want now?* Dreams are changing because our conscious awareness is moving upwards and once we clear a sufficient amount of unresolved residue, we might not have to interpret the symbols at all, just watch the resolution process and put it in motion the next day.

Dreams are becoming longer in sequence, or so it seems. Guide-speak says that is not true, it is just that I am remembering more of the dream because it wafts into my conscious awareness more than it used to. I can't remember the details just yet but I had one the other night that might explain it well. The dream will illustrate what I mean when I say Meander is spending way too much time trying to resolve every-day-life-issues while we move on to our next item on the To Do List. I am now asking Meander to refresh my memory so I can talk about it a bit. In this particular dream, my angelic wings were harder to find than they used to be when I knew I was dreaming.

At first remembering glimpse I recall someone dropping off four or five baby bears and they were around my campsite with five sleeping Scottie dogs. Now I am not particularly interested in dogs and dog breeds but I recognized these as the dogs pictured on shortbread cookie packages, whatever that might indicate. The truth be told, I was very concerned with moving both those sleeping dogs and the cute baby bears away from my camp site. And by the way, I don't like camping. However, I knew the bears and the dogs would both grow to be more than I could handle and would even provide an element of danger to my immediate surroundings. I also knew that the mindset I was working through was a temporary perception in that I was trying to repattern some old behaviors, which, come to think of it, probably accounts for the campsite since our mind is often symbolized by a house or a room within a house. In this case, a campsite would represent temporary housing, and to me personally, housing more primitive and unknown than comfortable, beautiful or happy.

"The bears were newly-developing habits of awareness, ways of looking at things around you. We were supplying the off-centered equation of hostility in your outlooks when approaching new and varied details of your mind and its surrounding elements."

They are indicating that they turned my emotional reactions on high so that my irritation became more developed consciously than it would have had I been able to stuff it down into the basement of my mind rather than deal with it as it cropped up. In my new way of looking at things, I would have to take any action possible to resolve the irritations rather than make a fictitious peace with the mishap. Now I know that is slightly difficult to understand but I also know I was working through self-behaviors that were somewhat immature – hence, baby bears. The campsite would indicate a temporary place of mental residence, thank god; who wants to live with bears? I remember now, we had just purchased a new car. Buying cars is my husband's job for more reasons than one; I am mostly concerned with getting from point A to point B with a car, but he has more interest in how we get to said points so cars are his baby. Basically, he did the dirty work and called me down to sign papers at the end of the deal.

So I arrived at the dealership and then waited around for the perfunctory stall while the business manager prepared the paperwork. I don't know what my husband was thinking because for some odd reason, our roles reversed themselves in that I became the one inspecting the paperwork details. Usually he played that role to the nth degree. After we finally set down to sign all the paperwork, the business manager spent a good deal of time touting a super-duper additional warranty and I began to wonder just how much extra we were paying for the unrequested add-on. The first number he gave us, as far as our monthly car payment, included this additional warranty. First I asked what the standard warranty covered as part of the original package and then how much the additional warranty added in cost. Since his answer was somewhat hazy, I asked him specifically what the payment was going to be *without* the additional warranty.

Instead of giving us a direct answer again, he said he could get us this new and improved warranty for only nine dollars a month. My husband and I both agreed that for $9 a month we would just take it. The process of buying this car took so long that by the time we were honing up the financing, we were too tired of the process to be fully aware of every little detail that might be bothering us.

To make a long story short, once we got home we looked more closely at the paperwork, because the business manager was just learning to use his new desktop-tablet-thingie to close the deal. His unfamiliarity with the technology served to side-track us more than usual, which made it difficult to focus on the actual numbers spelled out on the contract. After resting our minds enough to absorb the details of the paperwork, we saw that we had been charged for an additional theft system, besides the standard one that came with the car, and the $9/month warranty mysteriously totaled $1800 plus sales tax. It would take an eighteen-year car loan to pay that off at $9 a month. I could see my question of *what would the payment be without the warranty* had been ignored, and frankly, I am tired of corporate practices that are considered to be perfectly legal but surely less than ethical. There appear to be two sets of ethics in the corporate world and to compound the situation, this dealership is one of the local monopolies.

To further explain Meander's role here, the additional warranty was more than likely handled with less than the highest integrity but it was *my* role of 'irritated warrior' that had to be resolved and cleaned. Fixing the unfairness is not the issue but seeing it as unfairness is the glitch that causes a rift in our immediate emotional assessment. It is my *perception* of unfairness that the dream state seeks to repair. In the higher octaves of love, I would not have experienced the mild aggravation but rather simply returned to the dealership to correct what I would have interpreted to be a *mishap*. A love vibration allows others the freedom of learning/making mistakes. The underlying awareness is that everything is manageable, fixable and may even contain building blocks for something better.

That being said, I went over the numbers several times and decided that I was going to talk to the paperwork man again. I impatiently waited for the weekend to pass and made my call Monday morning. Another long story short, five calls later and about 8:00 that night he finally returned my call. When I asked about the theft system, he insisted it was a company standard that they perform themselves with every car, new or used, and that the salesman most definitely explained it. Not having been there for the hard sell, I wasn't sure but I knew the salesman was brand new and could easily have missed that point. Which leads me to another point, if it is standard with all your cars, why isn't on the sticker as part of the basic pricing? But I let that slide and addressed the issue of the warranty. I felt as though I were a naughty child or a bitchy wife that didn't want her husband to buy his favorite car when he finished with me and somehow, even though I reiterated that I asked for the amount of the payment without the warranty and was told a number that doesn't add up to $9 a month, he let me know I *my husband* wanted that warranty and it was worth $2800 and a good deal. I had the feeling he thought he was protecting my husband from me. Actually, it was my husband who pointed out the discrepancies; he just didn't want to make the call. And just so you know, unlike my visit to the emergency care clinic, I was the epitome of grace through this whole dialogue.

During this conversation, I was hyper-aware that there was a planet-wide flush moving through in regards to revenge and I was considering how far to push the envelope. Revenge is a concept that has become so interwoven into our thought patterns and belief systems that we are unaware of some of its most obvious placements in our ideologies. To explain, I once asked guide-speak why they didn't just tell those of us who can hear who the bad guys are and where to capture them – you know, psychics helping the police – it could be far easier than it is. I was quite surprised by their answer; they reminded me that our judicial system is based on revenge; that justice had somehow devolved to focus on punishment rather than the love-based reform that would truly resolve the situation. *"Many higher souls recommend that their charges be put on notice that their actions were incomplete in self-understanding and that they can heal self of the crime better than the interment required by your legal systems. The judgment of hardship is an issue long-held as required to satisfy repayment of wrong-doing when it further creates more of the same. Removing the revenge would require an understanding that the wrong-doer had been harmed enough that said reaction was a defense worth investigating and healing before the repayment began. Your society does not understand sufficiently that need for release of mind-pain nor its management."*

That being said, in effort to resolve my discord with the finance manager, I was walking a tight rope in trying to maintain a motivation of fairness rather than needing to win in order to curb my revenge-motivated anxiety. At what point does it become all about being the winner? We can handle the additional car payment and I was overly-cognizant of the process in that I didn't want to insist on winning but I did want to make the point that the practice was somewhat deceptive. Unfortunately for me, I let it go too soon. It kept bothering me…I had already missed a couple night's sleep over it and wanted it tied up in one of those pretty little packages to fit neatly on my shelf of *resolved to love*, but damn if that instant replay button wasn't still running. I was pissed off and unable to hold that love vibration I preach so much about.

I knew this dream pertained to my car-buying experience and to managing the thought patterns and behaviors, including those stemming from revenge-based reasoning, that I was trying to alter. This incident made it so easy to slip into old habits. I was overly aware of wanting to do whatever it took to ease my rewinding thoughts but knew well that this needed to be handled as correctly as possible in order for me to completely resolve it to love. Irritatingly, guide-speak clued me in they inserted the wave of *unsurity* within me so that I didn't push the envelope as far as I would have otherwise. This is tough because I really just wanted to say, "this isn't honest; I know this is how you do it and I know how it is to have to sell service contracts in order to make your bonus but I also know that they are not worth the money, at least not for us. We tend to be easy on things and find that if we pay as we go, it costs less than paying for the anticipation of something going haywire. At $9/month we were willing to let you make your bonus but for $27/month, we would have said absolutely not." I didn't expect him to change the contract, but I wanted to be heard.

In the dream, at least one of those bears was an irritation with the invisible faction for inserting a wave of fear that caused me to back off too soon for my own comfort in making my point. I have to get rid of that before it becomes a flaw in my perception again. Another of those bears had something to do with my getting angry over not being heard and becoming somewhat revengeful in that I would insist on *winning* in what could have quickly become a competition of wills. I am usually pretty good at not having to convince someone that my way is the right way but to have my perceptions negated caused a side of me to want to win the showdown. I was consciously working with that one. I had also been working with my husband in choosing the car, something I normally stayed out of but I am getting older and not really relishing the idea of climbing up in a man-machine. I had pushed the envelope farther than normal in stating my case for a less expensive and less impressive vehicle and since he finally came around, I seem to have been worn down in the envelope-pushing department. That was probably the bigger bear that was walking around the campfire looking for marshmallows – ewe, another thing I really don't like.

So the bears have the potential to grow bigger in my behavior patterns and I know they have to be removed but since I am so unsettled about this whole thing, staying in instant replay just feeds those bears. I have to resolve this in my emotional and mental fields. We also have the dogs to look at and as I write this, I am realizing that the reason I identified the dogs with the cookie package was because they were laying flat on their sides, like a two-dimensional photo of a dead dog with rigor mortis. I know they were aspects that I have worked through, irritating little facets of my behaviors that were in danger of returning if I couldn't work this out within my own mental and emotional confines. You know what I mean, something like spending all night telling the finance manager off in my mind, instead of sleeping. That kind of resolution does nothing but distort the original incident because your subconscious tries to find a way to replay it for you so you can make peace with the scenario. That level of frustration really requires some action in a rectifying direction to resolve it; action that does no harm nor makes the source of the conflict wrong but instead acknowledges the correctness of both sides and moves forward from that point. I knew that I had made great progress in pushing the envelope rather than habitually accepting what was dished out to me but this was one time I felt as though I hadn't pushed forward quite enough. That is one dog, maybe even two. I won't try to account for all the dogs but I can tell you that when the instant replay button would kick in, I would hear guide-speak whisper, *"let sleeping dogs lie."* I knew I needed to let this go, but how?

My usual format for this type of emotional conundrum is fast becoming a session with my favorite pillow and the couch. By the way, I say emotional conundrum for a reason, I could see the situation with sufficient mental clarity but could not seem to manage the raw feeling that drove the episode back into my conscious mind every time I tried to let it go. This is often where our layering of defense-based-subterfuge will begin to weave its way into our reasoning – thus dropping our rating on the love meter. In effort to avoid this old habit, I sprawled on the couch and asked to be raised an octave or two above my own fear-based residue, and to make direct contact with higher self. That means Meander's little quips were not my answer, they were echoing my own inner discord, just in case I missed it. I needed the top banana. I asked for help in resolving the less-than-love-based mincident that kept boomeranging back at me simply because it was not love-based. That's the thing, a love-based incident is used to fuel the world but a fear-based wave will keep coming back at you until it is resolved to a higher dimensional capacity. The energy is tainted and unusable so it winds up in our karmic bin of recycling.

The answer is usually not as apparent as guide-speak comments but comes through more quietly and seemingly from a farther distance. Sometimes I get nothing but a solution-based idea that will form later as I leave my focus to attend to something else. That is important – that is 'releasing my expectations' and that letting go is an absolute step in finding solutions or manifesting whatever it is you are working on. You have to release your expectations so solutions can form without your fear attached. It's like planting a seed and digging it up every five minutes to see if it sprouted yet. You have to let it go or it sprouts in the form of your fear *that it will not sprout*. I really needed to dive off the wave of emotion driving me through my repressed anger or I would begin to attract more of the same type scenarios. The wave we ride influences our perceptive windows; we will see one scenario as desirous if riding the higher wave, but the same scenario can be a curse if riding a wave of resentment.

This time I heard a definite voice of reason. Higher soul told me that my insecure wave of resonance caused a feeling of being unsure of my numbers, which caused me to back away from my argument before I had completely made my point. This is an issue, fear of being in error, that I had worked on and come through in many ways, but, sleeping dog that is was, it was back in a new form, indicating I am working on another aspect of fear-release where this particular behavior pattern will reassert itself if I don't manage to eliminate the pattern or perception. Also, I had another reason to stop my discussion because the business manager reiterated that he was doing what my husband wanted him to do and that caused me additional surge of insecurity since I had pushed to be included in choosing the car. I already felt a tinge of culpability because Ken didn't get his man-machine so the guilt aspect attached itself to my incorrect assumption that my husband would be unhappy with me if I crossed him again. I didn't cross him but that was how my unsure subconscious processed my reactions in this case. Another sleeping dog that almost woke up but as soon as I passed along the details of my conversation with the finance manager, I could see that Ken was in line with my thinking because he said, "*I* didn't want that damn warranty, who is he trying to kid?"

Then my quiet voice of reason said that I can talk about how this happened in the book and that would alleviate my sense of discord with the pseudo-ethics of our corporate mentality. I truly didn't want to cause harm to the salesman, a very kind man with six kids who surely needs the sale of that car. He had only worked there two weeks. What if he had been out of work before then? But, and here comes another bear and another sleeping dog; I have to admit, I feel as though I am being coerced by both the car manufacturer and dealership in that this kind salesman is graded on a survey that I must complete. I am to rate certain aspects of the car-buying process and the vehicle somewhere between one and ten, BUT, if I don't rate every question with a ten, he fails. To handle this experience without doing harm and to still be able to express my truth has me feeling like I am stuck between the proverbial rock and hard place.

I know these surveys are standard practice with some institutions now and I know that my brother's salary has dropped because of them. In his case, if the customer doesn't answer their phone after a certain number of tries, he also gets a zero in his customer service ratings. He used to make a nice little bonus based on those customer service ratings but the new rules make it easy to cut his income just a little more by purposely imposing specifications that are unlikely to be met. We know what they're doing and why, do they really think they're fooling anyone? In a love vibration, we would already be doing the best job we could and would not be concerned with such shallow marketing practices; but then again, the shallow marketing ploys wouldn't be in existence either.

I also knew that I should not want to cause harm to the business manager, after all, he is doing the job in the way they want him to and he is probably getting a bonus for selling that additional warranty. I've been there, I know how it is, but I also know I am not willing to pretend that it is okay. I need to have my say too. But here this survey now stares me in the face and I really don't want to keep the salesman from his bonus, nor do I want to encourage the car manufacturer to force me to say they are top-of-the-line in every possible way by giving them ratings of ten straight across the board. A conundrum that as of yet has not been resolved since I haven't completed the survey. I have, however, had the salesman calling the house, and more than once, just to make his case again for all tens, which I am sorry to say didn't help his case a bit. I refuse to lose anymore sleep over this but I do think my desire to resolve this situation is more involved than changing what happened. I have to make peace with all sides of the scenario by trying to understand the positions of each participant in a fair manner, before that bear gets any bigger and before that sleeping dog wakes up again. So I kind of know what that dream is about and I am working on a love-based resolution, which pretty much amounts to *accept the things that I cannot change* and to be content with the idea that I held myself up to my highest standards of integrity and grace.

In order for me to be able to employ the dream state as the rehearsal dinner that weds me to my creative desires, I have to clear enough of the in-box on the desk of my poor, over-worked subconscious so my whole dream state isn't taken up trying to get me off my duff to fix what I can fix (hence; deal with son's immature reactions to responsibility) and to accept what I cannot resolve without replaying it over and over. That's the thing; we are still working so many jobs in our subconscious realm of existence that getting one thing right is harder than it would be if we were available for night-time consultations with those that watch over us.

Our dream states are working over-time these days with additional assistance from our soul family in a way that amps up the resolutions going down in there. In all seriousness, it takes a while but we're making a significant amount of progress, progress that opens the door for several other dimensions of conscious awareness. Every time we are able to resolve even a little bit of the unresolved energy stored in our subconscious life recordings, resolve it sufficiently that it never returns as one of the little bears or sleeping dogs with the potential to become a behavior or thought pattern again, we are able to erase that wave of karmic residue from our Akashic history and move one step closer to graduation with a PHD in creating the circumstances we desire.

And here's an additional little tip on those dream state scenarios: ultimately, while in resolution mode, the character cast and all those symbols relate to changing our modes of thought and feeling to a more love-based vibration. The resolutions going down in the dream state pertain to corrections within the perceptive windows of our mind rather than the correction of what was or the behaviors of those around us. If your dreams happen to include your old ex-best friend acting out in the way that bothered you the most, you can darn well bet you're on the same wavelength in some area of your perceptions. If you are not riding a similar wave of energy, then you are learning to handle said wave of energy without doing harm, whether harm comes in the form of backlash or judgmental disapproval. That little tidbit is what makes the mirror theory so difficult to understand. If someone or something irritates you, the irritation is key that there is need for resolution or correction from within self. You may not be acting out in the way that bothers you but said behavior may have harmed you sufficiently in the past that there is need for further understanding and ability to make peace with the energy frequency, which means make peace with self in regards to past hurts. Once you understand the irritant behavior sufficiently that it no longer bothers you, it is no longer perceived as an irritation. You are finally at peace with one of the little bears in your dreams; one little bear that simply dissolves from your night-time mini-series dramas.

Thus far, this shift in consciousness has resulted in my hearing my guides consciously all the time. That includes my higher self when I seek a higher frame of reference, and I hear my guides of karmic responsibility when I am being shown how I created my own darn reality or why it is a little slower in dissolving. I hear my guides of karmic awareness when I require information already mastered in this plane of resonance during previous lifetimes and I may see guides of miracle-making when I ask for help in solving my current conundrums. Again, in case I haven't made this clear; these guides are all aspects of higher self, of our soul family. The most confusing voice for me is the Meander voice that articulates my inner-most feelings so that I can monitor those raw emotional reactions. For me, this is particularly necessary in that I am one of those left-brained, logicians that do not consider as much of the feeling center as what is necessary and what is needed at the moment. Now I get to explore all the emotional kerfluffle that I have spent a lifetime swallowing. At least it is being used to teach me what constitutes a love vibration and/or what exactly makes it a tainted-love vibration.

"But back to the drawing board of higher self – that's what it's all about in the dream state when you are trying to fix your life and create a better one than you already have, because first and foremost you for-got to be angry when you talked to your son. You had been previously re-wired to snap at those you love most when you lost your mind the first or 2nd time. Then when you slept you re-worked those wires in a way that amounted to your first or original way of saying – hey, what's going on with you? ... "

That's true. I have already mentioned that I used to be the world's greatest listener and that I was re-wired, so to speak, so that I am not as good at hearing somebody singin' the blues again. As I managed to quell the voice of snarky irritation in my mind and as I listened to the laments of the long-over-worked souls out there, I would find a change in what happened internally. I became more interested in heart-felt unity but not in the re-hashing of the dis-heartening event. I no longer chorale to my silent and invisible entourage 'help me to endure' or 'help me to find the off button' but I have learned to find a way to turn it off by myself.

At first I would find my mouth suddenly changing the subject in a way that felt almost rude as far as I was concerned. I recognized the guide-speak in my verbiage and I even felt their mergence into my thoughts and voice but at first I truly didn't expect the complete over-throw of my vocal kingdom. It wasn't that what was said was rude or even out of line, it was just that I was 110% aware that I didn't say it, and yet there it was – a rift in my dimensional portal of conversation that oh, so perfectly said 'sorry, we're not going there with you today.'

Those instances would happen in just the right times and places so that I quickly learned to peacefully segue to a less emotional topic, thereby being able to have some voice in the process so as not to de-plete my energy in whispering *help, I really don't want to hear about this again.* The truth is, the first few times felt slightly abrasive to me and probably more so to the speaker since they would not have been used to my disrupting their long-running train of thought. But my wiring is different now and I can't physically sit through the fight-or-flight purging that we have come to believe is therapeutic. A few good bouts of breath-related and dizzying anxiety finally clued me into action in subverting the on-going blues festivals.

I used to crave being listened to in that way. I have a friend who saw her therapist once of month just so she could speak her mind. She said she felt so much better afterwards that she was willing to pay to just have someone listen to her without criticism. I wanted that too. I actually made an appointment with a therapist to experience that process but it didn't work for me. The therapist actually had input and wanted to talk and she actually had things to say that let me know she wasn't focused on what I was trying to be heard about as much as why I felt the need to be heard. In a nutshell, she didn't want to hear me sing the blues and when all I wanted was to sing my blues I really didn't want to go any deeper to resolve the blues. I had hoped to find my comfort zone in singing my pain.

I guess it comes down to this; if you can't get to a point where you finally feel heard about something, then it is truly unresolved and requires some action on your part – usually. I was doing exactly what we all want when we're in an unresolved space of mind; "please-wave-your-magic-wand-and-make-it-go-away-because-even-telling-me-that-I-am-right-and-they-are-wrong-isn't-working-but-I-never-tire-of-hearing-it." It is a rhetorical place to be and no amount of talking about it will help. You have to change your wave of resonance.

"There is no one to do that for you but you DO know that it takes time to resolve some of the obstacles in your life."

True. So I began to learn to curtail my listening episodes. Not only was I unable to listen at length anymore, but I could see that going over and over the unfortunate events only served to re-energize a frequency of reality that attracts more hurtful episodes. After a while the singer will begin to see their whole life in terms corresponding to the one mishap that started their musical chorus at that moment. Most circumstances that result in a fight or flight emotional reaction will be riding a wave of victimhood resonance. Unfortunately, most cases of fight or flight emotional reactions are for something far less serious than life or death matters. For the most part, the blues singers have learned to dramatize their emotional reactions and or intellectual perceptions to gain external reinforcement. They make themselves victims so they can experience that external dose of mothering from anyone and everyone around them. The role of victim results from a hopeless feeling of having no choice or control in a situation. Once resolution makes some progress, victimhood loses its intensity as a feeling, and the feeling of possibility or manageability makes its way through the windows of perception.

For me, as listener to the newest blues renditions, I began to notice physical changes when I was starting to sink into that helpless feeling of not being able to escape the '*and then*' chorus. At first I would feel edgy, then a little light headed, and if that didn't clue me in to jump onto my new segue, I could always count on the Pac Man of Anxiety to begin to chew his way down my chakra system again. The resultant physical discomforts finally made it much easier to simply absent myself from the drama, with whatever means were available.

One of the changes that takes place during this shift in consciousness is that the dramatic feelings, whether from the positive or negative end of the emotional spectrum, will subside. There is a leveling out of the high drama of life that happens when you come into alignment with your own divinity. The truth is, once you connect to the knowing that there is a higher power up there watching you, you know that no matter what you encounter, you can handle it, but in the throes of fight or flight, you might not be so easily convinced.

As I have already mentioned, I had learned to swallow my verbal input to make way for calming the choppy waters that surrounded me. Suddenly, in the midst of my cycle of flush and rinse, I found my filters gone, lost in the whirlpool of belief systems and accompanying emotional residues. I could no longer sit through conversations without having some input that reflected who I am and what I thought. And if you weren't accustomed to considering what I had to say as having any significance, I just might bite your head off long enough to get your attention. There are those that accused me of menopause but *"we know this to be long ago done with you. Your surgery at age 33 took care of that side of emotional roller-coaster."*

Thanks for the support there; I needed to know that. So, as I was implying, that 'snapping to be heard' has been going on with me for a couple years now but it is finally receding. I had developed a pattern of discarding anything I had to say unless it involved placating the one in most need. These types of behaviors tend to turn to self-repeating patterns that will have to be *surprised* out of us. Take it from me; being snapped at from someone who never snaps is much easier than the swirly you might have to endure just to change an old pattern.

By the time you're snapping to be heard, if that's not your normal pattern, you will have endured endless mind-numbing chatter in the alternate-reality-dream-state until you have now consciously recognized a need for change in your own patterns. But what do you do when the family groups, and I am talking biological, work-based, friendship-based and even strangers on the bus type family groups, are used to you being the one with nothing to say? They may not hear you when first you try to insert a comment, and they may ignore you when you then clear your throat and raise your hand again, like you're in grade school. If all the quiet ways of becoming part of the conversation don't work because your pattern of being the quiet one is too well ingrained with those in your group, then you might just lose that filter between your random thought patterns and your mouth. You never know just what might pop out. I, myself, felt the queen of swords give birth to a hearty *shut up* more than once. Basically, what the guides were saying is that we have finally made enough progress in alternating family communication that I am being heard more and I can have my filter back, and you can have your head back if I mis-happened to have bitten it off.

In a more love-based reality, our thoughts connect as soon as our minds think about each other. As I understand it, our guides buffer that now until we get things cleaned up, but it is happening more and more - they're occasionally letting the connections be made. I now have to learn to quit thinking of people. First I had to learn to quit seeing myself as the center of the universe and then, just when I learned that I was looking at others first, I had to stop that too. I now understand that if we think of a person, we would, if not buffered, cause a rift in their conscious thought pattern. We would cause confusion by inserting our energy play list into the other party's auric field and vice-versa. Because we are buffered at this stage of the game, we are all safe from this end result, but if the buffering weren't there we would be creating havoc with those we think about from time to time. The ideal situation is that we think of ideas, causes, philosophies and sociological implications rather than a certain being or group. In divine mind, the only time another would be discussed, other than parenting, would be with said party present and involved.

I've heard from three of my five brothers in the last twenty-four hours. That usually means we're resurfacing after another biological swirly. I have a brother in Chicago, Steve, who moved away when he was about eighteen. He has considered coming back this way to be closer to my family for some time, and frankly, he is one of my best friends, so I spend a day-dream frame or two on his life, wishing he would just take a transfer with his job and be here.

A couple weeks ago I spent the night dreaming that my husband and I were in his apartment packing his things to move him back here. I kept waking up to go back to sleep and pack my brother's belongings and then to unpack them in his new place. In the morning my mind immediately thought about the night's dream pattern and guide-speak said, *"tell him."* I churned out a quick email describing the dream and forgot it. A couple hours later he called to say he had been thinking about doing just that the previous day. He fantasized that he would just get on the phone and say, "send the truck. I am moving in with you until I find a place." As an interesting side note, guide-speak had mentioned that it was important to tell him that my husband was helping us pack. He brought that up as well, saying he took it as a sign that Ken wouldn't mind if he took up residence here until he found a place to settle. The truth of the matter was that my husband, brother and I were all together in the dream state, riding the wheel of future possibility. There was need to resolve Steve's work dilemma and leaving the area to move closer to us fit well with his desires.

Our dreams are far more complex than our usual search for their meanings. We are by-products of a state of awareness that exists slightly closed off from our true potential. Our real consciousness is a multi-dimensional awareness that can operate from several places and faces of reality all at the same time. To understand your dreamland, you will have to understand further the make-up of your mind as well as your reality in terms of awareness that is about to expand beyond your current avenues of understanding. Dreams are a compilation of both subconscious attempts to resolve the unsettled moments of your day as well as the workings of your spirit self as you preview your immediate future to create a blueprint for things farther down the road. As you can see from my dream about my brother, the dream state can provide a side room to communicate with others in your life from an unconscious state where things can be resolved or worked through in regards to upcoming or current issues.

With the dimensional shift in play, we are all moving in a direction that allows us to tap into this higher level of insight on our own. This new paradigm will entail communication with our higher soul in a way that aids us in making responsible choices for our futures based on our highest integrity, once focused on the good of the group. It actually entails a reclaiming of free will in that we will consciously choose our path and take responsibility for it, all the while knowing we are capable of creating a new and more perfect scenario if required.

My brother's moving here is in his best interest for several reasons that I can see but it may not be his choice. For the past four or five years, every time my mind wanders in the direction of visualizing his move to this area, I hear, *"he doesn't want you to tell him what to do. He has other ideas."* That would usually divert my attention to something like *why am I so bossy with my brother?* Again, how embarrassing, but you get the drift. If I am making plans for you and my buffer zone isn't in operation, said plans might influence you in a way that wasn't in your best interest. It might rob you of your own ideas. All this requires a curtailing of my thought processes until sometimes I wonder what it is safe to think about – and how do I reach a point of being able to live in the moment and perhaps utilize my own dreams-cape vision board without moving into unauthorized air space?

A few years ago I sat in on one of my dreamscape visits to the wheel of high probability, which indicates that rather than me choosing a possibility and exploring how it might manifest, I would look at the lines of cause and effect around me to see what was already materializing. There were some issues that I was going to be facing soon and I was being clued in as to how to handle them. I was given three scenarios and told that there was a strong possibility that all three would materialize.

At the time my father just learned that he was in stage four of esophageal cancer and there was no treatment available so we knew the final outcome. During the session I was told was that no one would let me know if he took a turn for the worse or when he passed and that there would be no funeral services. That turned out to be true in the literal sense. We won't delve into that situation further except to say, you are correct, stemming from a family of divorce, I really wasn't in his life much except at the end where there was a short attempt on his part to include me.

The second scenario involved my mother. She was having some health problems at the time and there was some uncertainty in whether she was on her way out also. I was told that she was experiencing some heart trouble and would possibly be leaving at about the same time. I was instructed in how it would play out and when to take on the responsibility of respite care etc. There are seven of us and we all had different lessons to experience in this scenario so being clued in as to when and where I was needed was helpful.

My mother did, indeed, have some heart trouble and had a stint put in, but once that procedure was over, she was doing better than she had for most of her adult life. The truth is, she experienced a symbolic death in that her behavior patterns changed to someone who could enjoy the flow of life rather than hide from it. She was long-diagnosed as bipolar with long bouts of depression, something that was the norm since my early childhood and something that wouldn't surprise anyone given the circumstances of her situation. It is my new belief that her mental illness label will be peeling off at any minute.

This ride on the wheel of possible future events prefaced me with the occurrence both symbolically and literally, which was the result of my lack of healing in regards to my childhood situation. The residual negativity, or fear, would distort some of my interpretation, but the beauty of the wheel is that there is always the opportunity to change an outcome, which would have been, in this case, the result of my mother changing her lines of motivation, since I was previewing her situation. OK, to change the outcome would have been a possibility for my mother, had she previewed the situation. As for me, had I healed my own negative feelings, I would not have experienced this ride into our future with any symbolism. Dream state symbolism is a disguise for the fear. When we actually clear enough of the negativity from our perceptive windows to raise the vibration of mass consciousness, it will no longer be necessary for said fears to travel incognito through our attempts to resolve them to love. It will be safe to dip our conscious minds into the pool of disturbance without discomfort overload.

During these visits we look at the lines of cause and effect already in play, which means previewing how our emotional outlooks and our perceptions are causing our realities. These situations can and do change often since these previews also include guidance in making desired changes in the routing of the pathways of manifestation. A simple attitude of gratitude or the relaxing of a fierce determination can change future happenings almost instantaneously. In my case, there was a tendency to look upon my mother's health with a harsh reaction, so there was distortion in the way I translated. Rather than seeing the behaviors that tended to challenge me, I saw a symbolic representation of the wave my mother was riding at that moment in time. Her pathway was actually a wave of healing that wove its way into my wave of harsh judgment and presented itself as transition disguised as death.

The third scenario on the wheel that night turned out similar in that the symbolism peppered its way into my perceptions. I will have to mention here that in as much as this process is something that we currently experience while asleep, I was wide awake for this preview-series on the Ferris- wheel of possibility. This process stems from superconscious awareness and it is part of the dream state and the consciousness evolution we are heading for now. Instead of leaving our subconscious and superconscious work up to the unconscious make-up of our mind, we are fast becoming involved in the big stuff. Should it be necessary, we will actually have conscious recall of our *trips to the wheel*, as I have come to call them.

So, moving back to that third scenario, we threw the dice again onto the wheel of future possibility. My brother, Steve, has experienced an illness that was medically pronounced as terminal but he long ago by-passed the extreme danger area. Over twenty years later he is still with us and doing much better now; however, during this time he was going through his own subconscious areas of resolution and was very worried that he might lose his job and even worse, his insurance. During this trip to the wheel, the invisible voice told me that my brother might very well lose his job soon and that it would probably be necessary to move him here. They instructed me in exactly what to do during the move; what to throw away and what to keep and how to go about the entire move with very little stress. Another interesting point worth mentioning is that he also desired to move to a newer apartment.

Soon after this little preview of possibility on the wheel of prophesy, my brother's bedroom ceiling caved in and he had to move to a newer, more recently renovated apartment within his building. He didn't lose his job but he did get to move. The whole process went pretty smooth since things simply fell into place for him as far as him manifesting his dream of the new apartment. I told him what I had been shown in the vision of his move and he had already come to the same conclusions and was proceeding in exactly that manner. It was time for him to re-pattern in a big way since his illness had caused him to see life as a short-term package. In truth, his health had become quite manageable and rebuilding his outlook with a new environment made it all that much easier – and fit into his wishes perfectly. It is quite normal to crave a move in location during periods of shift in mental consciousness. That is how the desire to change or modify one's mental perceptions will manifest in the physical.

There is some symbology in the way these scenarios came down. All three involved a death of some kind. In Steve's case, the death was of his perception that he was waiting to die. Instead, he would repattern with his life ahead of him, rather than behind him. My mother may have been in flux at the time as to stay in the physical or just move on, but she chose to stay, with her new and improved life force. I have to say that her mental and emotional outlook improved greatly, thus pulling her into a new and healthier flow as well. My father, who I never knew all that well but liked, passed on, but it was that experience that higher self used to teach me how the process really works – well – at least as far as I know. Maybe I should say it was the beginning of the collapse of my new age belief systems as far as how things work between us and spirit. Guide-speak used that event as a way to show me what happens as we leave this dimension of existence and also to make the point that my father would *not* become one of my spirit guides. And PS, during my final editing of this book, Steve's job was eliminated and he is, indeed, moving in with us until he finds his own place.

The other day I was doing some cleaning and my mind kept naturally gravitating towards other people and events. I was yanked back to now every time with a twist or turn in the thought that somehow made me guilty of unfair comparisons. My intent wasn't to go in that direction and I quickly realized there was some hijacking of the train of my thoughts. They were showing me a thought pattern that needed to change. The really unfair part was that I wasn't in comparison mode but they kept throwing my thoughts in front of that old train and the only way to save myself was to jump off the track and have a short discussion with me – whoever the whole *me* was at that moment.

That process, part of the reprogramming of our subconscious' attempts to connect the dots in old emotionating patterns, is begging for a rewiring using new and updated equipment, i.e., happier moments to cling to until we learn how to stay in the moment. Some of the techniques used there are the visits to the Wheel of Future Probability and Possibility. They will infuse short synapses of these happenings into our waking awareness so that we feel as though something good is about to happen – or something not so good. Either way, it creates a sense of expectation, which in turn serves to attract us to whatever train is passing by on the matching gravitational track or resonating energy field. All that means is this: we are allowing our past to influence our presence far too much and in a not so good way because we are gravitating towards old patterns of feeling. I only mention this so that should you recognize that happening just when you're trying not to talk about the people that trip your trigger, you will know that you're not losing your mind, you are trying to realign with more positive emotional patterns. Change the thoughts to happy-mode; it helps.

To give you a better idea of the Wheel of Prophesy, such as the wheel of high probability, this afternoon I picked up my son from work and we were trucking down the road talking about his day when I noticed that the traffic, not particularly heavy but slightly jammed up, was moving sporadically and yet more slowly than necessary. The car in front of me seemed to be dogging it and the car right next to me was aggressively tail-gaiting a truck ahead of him and jamming on his breaks every few seconds. He was seemingly suffering a good bout of road rage and I found his company uncomfortable and I slowed a bit so I wasn't in his line of fire. At that point, guide-speak pointed out that the car in front of me was feeling some stress from my closeness and that they had asked me subconsciously to ease off as the driver was swirly-stressed and her sensitivity knob was turned up on high. My son pointed out that Mr. Road Rage was really angry and looked as though he were telling all of us where to go. I remember thinking that he was an accident ready to happen when the invisible faction said, "*yes, he is not opposed to that. Move back a little more.*"

I had been pushing a little hard myself because I didn't want him cutting in front of me again, as he had been jumping from lane to lane, but I eased back and gave him room just in case he chose to slide right over top of me. Then I asked guide-speak if there was a problem. They said that he was feeling as though he couldn't handle things; he was smack dab in the middle of a swirly with pounding heart and intense anxiety levels and his higher soul would allow him the mishap of a fender bender to slow him up if there were others of us six cars coming from a similar wave of motion. They said, "*we are all together up here and none of us wants this mishap so we are dispersing the jam in a way that slows him up but doesn't cause injury or damage to any of you.*"

I stayed back and noticed a couple other odd moves by the cars he tried to pass in the traffic cluster. He seemed to get ahead of one car only to meet circumstances that caused the same car to move around him again. He truly was making no headway in moving through a now-down-to-five-car-jam. As far as I followed him, his road rage appeared to continue but he sure wasn't getting very far with the traffic. The interesting thing was that traffic really wasn't busy; he just couldn't get past a small cluster of cars.

I didn't hear from the other drivers' higher souls, nor would I have needed to, but I was able to discuss the situation with my higher self and to be clued in on the monitoring of the wheel of high probability in play so as to know more of what I was involved in and how best to realign myself right back out of it. I found it interesting that all drivers were consulted, at the level of higher soul, as to whether or not to allow Mr. Angry Man to bump our vehicles or not. Note to the wise, however, the information given during this incident is not typical, nor is it the way we get into or avoid car accidents. Guide-speak has asked that I explain that although they monitor us closely, they really do not get so involved in our *day-to-day trafficking,* but in this case they opted to answer my internal concerns in a way that could be used to explain the wheel of high probability.

There was a lot less responsibility with feeling good before I had to monitor my word, thought and deed stuff PLUS make sure my intention allowed for the good of the group. I have had a hard time finding my rhythm in this chapter until I finally decided to sit down and meditate to seek some clarity. Truth be told, I don't always meditate as much as I just lie down and allow the patterns of the subconscious residue to emerge. I become cognizant of this at about the alpha state, just before I turn my conscious mind over to sleep. Have you ever noticed when you reach that point that you seem to be listening to a conversation or hearing someone explain something that makes perfect sense and suddenly you feel jerked awake and have no idea what you were just listening to? Other than it made sense a second ago…

That's part of what I am talking about. It can be a snippet of your subconscious trying to reason through something that is beginning to simmer a little too much on that backburner again, or it can be some superconscious reasoning coming through from an aspect of higher self that allows resolution at a coded time. It is the beginning of bringing our dream state into our conscious mind where we can take control of the issues and how they are filed. The other day I had a client who said, "I am starting to dream before I even go to sleep." Yes, we are! That's where we have an opportunity to be more involved in the subconscious-resolution-stage, which gets us to the design and build app even quicker.

I shall call my higher self *Ecknoreial* now since she spent so much time encouraging me to search for her – that way my search counted for something. So Ecknoreial planted a seed in my subconscious just then, something like in the movie *Inception*, only a whole lot less violently, that would emerge in my conscious awareness at a coded moment. I have watched her do some of this gardening during my night stints with her. She showed me how she would infuse an understanding into my awareness once a certain code word or name came up during my waking states. That's where that conversation from the alpha state comes in; she is explaining and then pulls the awareness until the frequency alarm goes off. The future incident she used as an awakening point was taken off the wheel of high probability with the knowing from the gates of unveiled consciousness, that's us while in the love vibration of spirit, that at a certain point we would be ready for the seed to sprout. The name Ecknoreial was one such code that was planted within me long before I became aware of how all this works. When I finally had conscious contact with the name, the sense of familiarity was so strong that I knew I was onto something important. I was, I was onto a wild goose chase, but it was fun while it lasted.

That is just one thing that might be happening from the proverbial alpha state, and truth be told, I get a lot of my best material then. The other possibility, as I've already mentioned, is that simmering pots and pans are beginning to splash gunk on the stove of my subconscious. I have learned to tune in on these episodes more now so that if I catch some of the errant reasoning, I can move in with my conscious mind and address things so that they might be filed under closed in love or at least closed until further action can render them harmless.

There are several ways this happens. Sometimes I just notice the cartoons that begin to form from the wafting energy in there. Now the truth is that I am getting help from Ecknoreial there in that she will say a word as I watch the formation of the vision and that word points me in the direction from whence came that little fat lady holding in her stomach. So just before her feet become elongated and too narrow to hold her up, I realize she has something to do with me and the way I am seeing myself again. If I can see the error in the reasoning, I can ask Ecknoreial to help me correct it. Sometimes things are not clear to me and I just observe and let it go. Sometimes I find myself answering an invisible question out loud or spelling a word over and over until my conscious mind grabs it and throws it into my waking awareness. It is usually coded and key to something I am asking about or for.

One interesting aspect of this semi-awake state is that I can watch good ole' Ecknoreial create the visions. I can see the energy just moving around and then she says a word and the light shapes begin to take form. The visual may continue to become more clear, or simply dissipate, as she instructs it. Creative energy is exactly that – we are creating those forms with our thoughts all day long. And our over-worked subconscious is creating some snarling little bears too. Is it any wonder we have to be buffered?

We are at a point in bleed-through awareness, meaning the veil is lifting but not gone yet, so that there can be confusion as to when we are awake and when we are asleep. Our conscious mind is at a point where it wants to be further involved in all these things that are cordoned off and it is beginning to retain snippets of what is happening in the veiled off portions of our awareness. We are remembering our dreams longer and more clearly as well as experiencing more of the déjà vu that results from our night visits to the wheels of possibility and probability. Ecknoreial uses this sometimes confusing drifting between dimensions as prime time to plant seeds of peace and/or unrest should we require a nudge on the duff to get moving.

That couch I lay on has become the harbinger of some pretty interesting waking dreams. One afternoon I lay down and sorted through some the pre-alpha gunk: that is when your mind is just yakking atcha' when you first try to relax. After that I must have fallen asleep because all of a sudden I woke up. The couch faces three adjacent windows that look out past the backyard to a wooded area. As I looked outside I saw the black and white humming bird that usually hung out there. It was suspended at the window just long enough for me to look at it when it suddenly flew right through the window – glass, screen and all – and fell down behind the drape.

I thought, *oh crap,* how am I going to get that bird outside without hurting it. I had visions of it flying frantically through the house, more like an angry raccoon than the harmless little humming bird it was. I got up and walked ever-so-gingerly to the drape and pulled it back to see if the bird was ok when I saw a little black and white fairy about the size of a Barbie doll with the very same markings as the humming bird. She was getting up off the floor and she looked up at me. Noticing the dust bunnies behind the drape and not knowing exactly how to address a fairy, I said, "hi, who are you?" She said "Iotta" and with that I woke up and thought *I aughta' dust.*

My conscious reasoning mind was so involved in that dream that I had no clue I was dreaming. I was used to a whole lot less reasoning ability when I knew I was dreaming – even though there was always a good portion of my reasoning trying to seep through. A lot of times, before the flush, when dreams were that pronounced, there was usually an effort by the Ecknoreials of our soul to fuse them into our waking state because there was superconscious significance in the dream scenario. That was usually an indication that our spirit self was leaving us with a message – one that hopefully we would come around to understanding better than when we first awakened.

During the flush, which, by the way, is an on-going thing for at least our immediate futures, our dream states are waking up to include more of our conscious minds. That means that Meander's least insignificant wanderings may show up in Hollywood bright lights upon awakening. Because it is so real, you may apply more significance to her attempt to clean up your coffee spill on the beige carpet than necessary. If Meander is cleaning the spill, it is probably bugging you and you should just get up and scrub on it a little harder, but if Ecknoreial is referencing the spill, the symbology indicates there is a problem in the ways you choose to ground yourself, i.e. – *how do I make myself comfortable with me and the world around me?*

"There is more to it; Ecknoreial wants your own floor clear of residue so you can create the you that you want to become."

Got it; thanks for the direction and further reference to my private flush of the fear. Cleaning rooms or houses in our dreams indicates we are cleaning our minds, so suffice it to say there is no clear way at this juncture to know if you are clearing residue with Meander or gardening with Ecknoreial, but your *pure* intuitive side will give you a clue if you need it. Pure intuition is when your love vibration is high enough to bypass the lessons of the karmic individual, and by the way, karma isn't something you have to repay as much as it is simply needing to understand the error in your reasoning or your feelings. The best advice I can give you here is that if you feel a sense of urgency, that is not Ecknoreial – wait a while and see how you feel. This can take up to a couple weeks or longer if you are shedding unwanted baggage in the underground flushing system. True messages from Ecknoreial will have a sense of peace with them. If the area in the dream is dark and dirty, you can about be sure you are looking at Meander's garbage disposal. If the accompanying background is bright and hopeful, hang on to the feeling, it will lead somewhere and Ecknoreial is probably behind it in some way. Those can be the prophetic dreams we're all hoping for.

As a post script I want to add one more thing here, and that is that dream symbology, from my point of view, is a unique code between you and your Ecknoreial and your Meander. At some level of awareness you will know the meaning of what you need to know. It is possible to ask your mind to use the symbology laid out for you in someone else's book and it will comply at times, but there will always be times when only you know the meaning of the dragon in your dreams.

Now, onto other dimensions of possibility from the dream state; your dream state can be used as your own private vision board, complete with unlimited potential to create your hopes and dreams, all without the confines of creating mega-mistakes. That means with your conscious mind and right now; you don't have to wait for the next sleeping session to meet with Ecknoreial and the gang. Once we move enough of Meander's cleaning duties out of the way, we can access that design and build app while we navigate our day. Think of that potential as the wheel of possibility. Using that design and build app is the real meaning of lucid dreaming. In lucid dreaming we are really not asleep at all but awake in a heightened state and accessing the drawing board in our mind. We create our wishes and dreams in a rehearsal mode and throw them on the wheels of possibility and probability to explore the differing ways things can play out. Once we're satisfied with the results, we go to work in the world of form to practice that elusive concept of manifestation.

The wheel of high probability is the one Ecknoreial used to keep me from playing bumper car with Mr. Road Rage. The truth be told, she rolls the wheel as necessary while I am alive down here in Angst-town. She really does not interfere in what is playing out unless required and encouraged by divine law.

"Ecknoreial is always there now but there will come a time in the evolution of consciousness where you play the wheel from right where you sit – the here and now."

"When we speak of blueprints of manifestation we are speaking of possible events or happenings that might initiate the changes we want to see and be rather than a plan we made for your life's journey."

Thank you. The blueprint analogy shows up a lot when I do a reading. It tells the client that they are previewing something new in regards to different possible ways of solution or accomplishment. It clues them in that there is an answer or a divine design up there waiting for the right time to present itself, so that they feel the hope they need to raise their energy up an octave or two and grab it. When this happens, they create a seeming vortex of energy that matches their hope and serves to attract like-minded frequencies of possibility. The really cool thing is, a little way down the road, we will be able to preview this and have conscious input into our life designs, rather than hoping some of the magic will stay with us once we wake up. We won't have to try to remember to keep those confusing dream journals.

In the creative visualization exercises I learned about a hundred years ago, where I tried to teach myself how to become a metaphysical guru in one easy lesson, I would spend some quiet time in a hopefully-productive, meditative state where I would try to get as close to the alpha state as possible without falling asleep. In these lessons, once you hit that darned-near hidden realm of possibility, especially if you're already tired from running the house and the job, you instruct your mind in daydreaming, so to speak, about whatever it is you want to create. In truth, I always found this process to be a luxury that I rarely had time to indulge in, and since my non-productive daydreams were always trying to make myself thinner, I can't really say I've had much luck in this portion of my self-imposed seminars. Now I realize that I was trying to hit that wheel of possibility but my subconscious piles of dirty laundry were getting in the way of my relaxed, love vibration. The other part of that non-equation is that my desire base was the result of too many fear-based motivations, a little aspect of creation that the wheel of possibility helps us to fix.

The biggest differences between now and then are that I now understand that the intention must be from the heart, not mimicking the ideal. Then I have to make sure the end result is good for the group. Both the intention and the desire should have no harmful consequences for anyone, so I suppose that means refusing to feed your kids just so you don't inadvertently shove a spoon of peanut butter into your mouth is out of the question. Your desire should not be in making anyone wrong or in changing their life circumstances – only your own. And here's the trickiest part; how far can you go in applying these hints to your everyday circumstances? Those are good clues as to when you're holding a love vibration that is high enough to create a flaw-free desire. The higher your love vibration is, the better your creation. If you're holding too much fear in your desire, you will have to resolve the fear-based issues before you see much in the way of results. Another little clue there; oftentimes the desire will change as the fear is resolved.

So what happens when we want something? Let's visit the wheel of possibility; let's try some lucid dreaming as it takes place during the shift – where we are learning to use the higher realm connections and still operating from a physical standpoint as well. I wanted to give

122

a class or workshop at a particular business in my area that thus far hadn't been open to my services. An hour or two after I penciled them in on my-most-wanted list, a running list I use to clarify my desires, they called and asked me to do a workshop on manifesting via the vision board. Now I have to tell you, I am not big on making art per se; I would rather enjoy someone else's work. I wasn't sure what to say when I realized that my most-wanted-list was the beginning of a trip to the wheel of possibility and just explaining how our minds work in regards to this process and how to get there using lists, visuals, or even affirmations would be a more complete workshop than working with glue and poster board, something I really don't relish. When I included this business on my most-wanted-list, my intentions and desires were aligned with their needs and the surfing angel in the sky sent them my way.

Using a list to clarify my desires is highly effective and warrants a bit more in way of explanation. It's easy and has amazing results. Just brainstorm away and write down ten things that you desire, anything from material items to changes within your mental and emotional make-up. Organize them with some degree of care as to what is most important to you. The rest is easy, just three times a day read the list and put it away. Yes, read it – you're saying *hey universe, here's what I am creating,* then put it away and forget it. Putting it away amounts to releasing your expectations in terms of the end result, and that is an important step in creation because you are releasing any hidden fears that may be tied to the desire. It will keep you from manifesting the fear. It is amazing what can happen. Sometimes you begin to take steps towards something you've been procrastinating about and sometimes you begin to realize that some desires have lost their appeal. That's good; you're getting to the root of your true desires and motivations. Just go with it and take the time to re-do the list about once a week.

That in itself is very productive but later I added a page of affirmations that I had taken the time to write out, all written in such a way that the highest and best good of the group was at the forefront. They quickly became a mantra I used when driving to work. Something about saying them in the car provided me peace and they easily became a habit that needed to happen for me to feel complete. I didn't realize until later, when someone asked how I came to hear my spirit guides, and guide-speak clued me in, that the affirmations I spoke were designed to align my outward self with conscious spiritual communication that would be of service to others. The words I spoke brought my vibration in alignment with the desires behind the affirmations. And yes, guide-speak was instrumental in pushing me in that direction with the creation of the affirmations. Both the list and the affirmations served as a prayer to pave the way for my creations.

As the swirly residue clears, we can better understand our true desires and how they motivate us. Learning to tune into our desires now is difficult because they are hidden below the layers of fear-based strategy we use to make our way through a culture filled with fear-based protocol. Our dream state is a dimension of possibility that exists for us to learn to design and manifest our reality, to play creator with our own god-given capabilities. That is why we're here. That's what we came to learn. The fly in the ointment is that until we can clean the unresolved gunk from the basements of our mind, we cannot access the drawing board that allows us to design our desires, at least not consciously. We keep it continually in motion just resolving the moments of our lives where we slip out of love. Once the basement of our minds is clean and Meander comes up to converse with us during the day, while we clear as we go, we can take that class in divine design and begin to manifest the beauty of life that stays hidden just behind the secret doorway of our conscious awareness. And I'll tell you another little secret; once the fear is cleared, the subconscious mind and the superconscious mind are really all part of the same penthouse suite, a suite where we can access the higher realms without all the guess work.

CHAPTER 6

DANCING WITH SPIRITUAL VERTIGO

I want to know at what point energy becomes consciousness. Everything is energy but is it always conscious energy? If all energy carries with it a form of consciousness, how does it evolve to a point of consciousness as we know it? Those are the kinds of thoughts I am always having but since I get no cooperation from those who can certainly see further than me, I give up and direct my thoughts to something easier for me to see. Like a chocolate soda...

In deciding which direction to take this chapter, I have to wonder, why does the information I want seldom come from discussions with the guides? Sometimes they cooperate but the answers have usually permeated my conscious awareness well before guide-speak gives me the verbal cues. Right now I know that I should expect zilch in the ways of collaboration as far as new material because I am in the throes of another swirly. The next month or two could be full of swirlys, unfortunately. There is this planetary alignment thing going on and our higher selves, as well as the council that acts as higher self for the planet as a whole, that would be the galactic council thingy, will make some adjustments in our personal frequencies that will improve the vibration of mass consciousness. That means our love meters are expected to move upwards, folks, and we will have to raise our own mental and emotional acumen to exist comfortably. I have come to know that during these episodes, I will experience a series of road blocks and physical owies that keep me from getting where I want to go.

Alright, at this moment the PacMan-gnawing-anxiety-syndrome is upon me again but I know that there are likely to be many such adjustments over the next week or so. This concerted effort to raise the vibration of mass consciousness incorporates more of the quickening where we are only beginning to see, feel and hear how our thoughts are creating our world. The time delay is off in more ways than one. There are times scheduled for our vibration of mass consciousness to move upward and if we're not ready for the degree or two of rise, we will experience some physical discomfort as we bob for air during our swirlys and then take a swim through the gelatinous atmosphere of our lives while we move through the slowness of repatterning our aware-ness. By the same token, our own personal vibration, which amounts to our framework of mental and emotional references, our perceptions of us and the world around us, will experience a divine shift also. I am shifting again, and may I just say - ouch!

I spend way too much time and energy trying to identify my areas of shift. That is the drawback in learning how this process works. I am overly aware of its nuances. That is exactly why we don't know which areas of our fear-based reality are in shift – we would put too much attention there and create more fear because our fear that we are not doing it right would permeate the pile of clean laundry pulled from the piles of files seeking resolution. Our fear of failure would taint the clean stuff even as we repattern.

There are things happening out there that defy all logic as we have known it. These strange emotional outbursts and unusual disagree-ments happen as that vibratory rate is pulled up rather than allowed to float upwards of its own volition. If we could naturally transcend our areas of weakness, we would casually – woops, I mean causally - learn our lessons and be the better for it. But for now, we are being asked to move through the accelerated process of realignment and it causes some whoopsies when we realize that our filters of reasoning have been misplaced.

We are at a turning point in awareness where we are taking con-scious control of our minds. As that happens, whatever is bothering us takes on a magnification emotionally as well as a strong urge to move forward. The combination of the two areas, that of needing to move upward in resonance of love and the need to solve that which churns within as a problem become entangled. That urge is somewhat distorted by a need to resolve the fear-based situation in a hurried way and there are times when there is a bleed through in our minds as to possible solutions and the fear-based scenarios that spring up during the flushing of fear. These situations can prove to be mind-bending as well as mind-opening. The interim of discomfort can be more than slightly disquieting and can bring with it an assortment of physical aggravations, anything from joint pains to digestive dilemmas and mind-draining headaches – most of which will dissipate once you round the corner of repatterning the swirly in process. The trick is to learn to recognize your swirly patterns and then take your time about going to visit the local surgeon. The doctor can provide you with symptom-management, should you prefer that route, but if there is a small voice of reason somewhere deep within telling you this isn't going to last or this isn't serious, just hang in there for a while before you take up with the major league procedures.

During one of my more intense swirly-power-washes, I had a visit to the ER to address my PTSD-like symptoms and my inability to take a decent breath of air. The ER doctor ordered an ultrasound to see what might be causing the pressure in my chest area, apparently they had ruled out heart attack, and he noticed gall stones. He dismissed me with the name of a surgeon and told me I really should have my gall bladder out. I am not expecting him to understand my situation; this was emergency care and other than the two times mentioned in this book, I have not taken that route for thirty-plus years. The truth was, the doctor confirmed that I wasn't having a heart attack and that was my biggest concern, so I threw the surgeon's number in the trash. I have been aware of my gall stones since my early twenties and I have an internal sense that tells me if I am starting to heart-burn or gas-pain up, to lay off all food intake for a while and drink warm water if I feel pain. The truth is I don't have to do anything special very often but when I do, the symptoms tend to heal quickly, so I see no reason to go under the knife, or laser, as the case may be. Health care professionals will use a different set of belief systems than me and my invisible faction, but either set will work if that's where your beliefs reside. That's the thing about taking conscious control of your mind, you have more ability to create your own reality. Trading in the belief systems that keep us strapped financially or walking a tightrope of discipline that prevents us from *living in the moment* – a true sign of love vibration – are really possible.

I am going to take this reasoning a layer farther than just self-healing. My course of study with the invisible entourage has included a lot of new understandings in regards to the vibration of mass consciousness and how the fear in our perceptions and emotions really changes our picture of reality. As the fear-flush does its work in purging us of long-standing negativity, we require less in terms of self-nourishment. That means less food, less sleep – which is not to be confused with the sleeplessness of the swirly – and less self-centered focus. Before the drop in our love barometers, way back before forest primeval, we, as a species only required food sustenance as children. Once we were full-grown, we ceased to eat at all other than the occasional drink of water. The need for food came later when the fears began to distort our concepts and abilities. As our minds tired of processing the negative energy patterns, resolving our energy to the clean, reusable state, our physical bodies began to require replenishment in terms of more earth. Our bodies are of the earth and were beginning to break down quicker due to lack of harmony in the energy that circulated between beings. Before that time, breath and a little water did the trick. With the clearing of the fear, we will begin to notice that we require less and less food again; however, that is true if we can make eating a positive experience, rather than fear-based; and over-focus on prevention is fear-based. To make eating and food a focus of finding-the-errors only serves to compound the issues in the swirly-clearing-house and makes us want to eat more than we would if eating were a non-issue.

The guides explained that the stress of the dream state swirly does a number on our gall-bladder and kidneys and other stress-processing organs. Poor Gluten, all those sharp gas pains and digestive bloating that come part and parcel with almost every swirly are giving 'ole Gluten-burg a bad rap, and causing extra stress on our already shaky bank accounts and our overly-obsessive guidelines on what is safe to eat. As we flush the fears behind our errant reasoning and behaviors we will mesh well with the world around us, and so will our gall-bladders and kidneys.

Since my early swirly days, I have learned a bit more, like what mind sets for me, personally, causes those lymphatic taxations. And if those issues aren't a part of my conscious existence when the breath-less-syndrome occurs, before I call the health-care professionals, I make sure there isn't another new swirly in process where new layers of behaviors are being flushed. That swirly is a stressful process since portions of it are a quite literally a bad dream with no ability to wake up until a certain amount of progress is made in our subconscious rea-soning. This causes some physical manifestations of dis-ease that will resist symptom-management until, as I mentioned before, we round the corner in repatterning the errant understandings. It takes a little longer than you might think since we have to repattern not only how we are looking at things and acting out but also how we react emotionally. There is an actual training session we move through in addressing our immature feelings in a way that tells the self they are inappropriate and no longer acceptable. Many of the physical discomforts that occur at that point will kick in just as the errant emotional reaction triggers. Call it guide-based behavior reinforcement if you will; it bites but it works. The days of accepting our personal immaturities as our claim to individuality or the result of a mother that criticized too much are long gone. Your entourage will no longer make it comfortable for you to stay in that mode of rationalization. Every time your mind and feelings resort to that old paradigm of justification, you may experience a tap on the head or a not-to-be-ignored gas pain, a little tidbit straight from spirit just to get your attention moving in the right direction, and once the actual redirection begins in changing the set pattern, the quickening sets in and you manifest the accompanying heart-burn or shoulder pain. Many of these symptoms will dissipate and quickly once your mind is beginning to flow in the higher frequency of love – which happens almost without notice. A good sign you are on the road to recovery is when you notice something that usually irritates you *isn't.*

Which, incidentally, brings up another point; one of my most prev-alent symptoms during this process is that of allergy-like responses to anything and everything; nothing serious, just itching and sneezing and runny nose kinda' stuff. We are really not becoming allergic to the world around us nor are we creating virus' capable of traveling through the phone lines to greet us, but we are learning to live with our heart-sensitivities turned up a little higher so that we can discern when we are having less than mature emotional reactions to the world around us. The key here is to remember that it is not the world we have to change but our emotional reaction to it and all its creatures – even the stink bugs that seem to have nowhere else to be but in my house.

During the swirly process your reasoning may not be up to its usual standards of genius-level thinking. When you notice you're making stupid mistakes in the checkbook or you're turning right and using your left signal again, slow your bootie down. This is prime time for a misplacement of the filter of reason that helps us determine where we really are on the scale of pragmatic idealism.

A good example of this bleed-through is the sudden urge to give away the farm. As you round the corner on the swirly pattern in play, you will begin to notice what appears to be an upsurge in materialistic comfort. Good, you are beginning to notice the blessings around you rather than the disappointments. Then, in keeping with your newly washed motivation, you have an urge to solve world hunger all by yourself and hand over your next paycheck to the food bank. A very noble gesture and one that will be appreciated by those on the receiving end and by those that watch over us, but you may feel a slight pinch when the rent comes due and you fear you have made a big mistake. The solution is there in the middle; you don't have to give it all away, keep enough to allow self-freedom of worry and still make allowances for the good of the whole. It's just a matter of learning to find the balance, but the first couple episodes can leave you wondering where your reasoning mind went when you decided to save the world.

For many of us, we will simply have an overwhelming desire to volunteer; volunteer for whatever cause resonates with us at that time. I, personally, began to fantasize about buying a house for everyone tied to me that could use a little financial break. That tells me I feel somewhat strapped by our mortgage; something I am making peace with as we speak. An interesting side note in my dreams of winning the lottery was that the entourage reminded me that everyone has their own guidance and their own lessons and to buy them a house may not be their best solution. I suppose it boils down to realizing this mode of thought is the beginning of a motivation that includes the good of the group, but the solutions that come through me at this stage of the game are still tied to my fears. Again, slow your bootie down before you try to end world poverty all by yourself; once the urgency dissipates, better solutions are available.

Just slightly before or after that stage of swirly management, your thoughts go through a period of adjustment where they appear to take on a mind of their own and are hijacked to places unknown. You're about to learn more about your own personal, however-well-hidden, jackass within. I would give you some well-known examples but I am going to refrain so as not to do harm to some of our super stars and politicians. We're all doing it, they're just doing it publicly.

At this stage you're usually knee-deep in dirty subconscious wash-water that requires a sump pump of much larger proportions than your current installation. There is a back-up of ganoopies that may infiltrate your solid good reasoning faculties. STOP, look and listen. That strong urge to move upward on the love barometer is attaching itself to the issues being flushed. You may be trying to empty the pot that's almost soup, or to sell your house for a fraction of its worth because it is inhabited by spirit bogeymen.

During one such episode I was driving six hours north of here after having worked with my husband at a trade show. The plan was that I would leave him and travel north another couple hours to visit my mother. Although I am much better about it now, I had some pretty silly fears regarding driving out of my comfort zone. I had also experienced a good bout of swirly-related sciatic nerve that had kept me from driving comfortably for almost a year. I was just coming out of that healing, one that had left a good share of scar tissue in my driving-field of vision.

I was doing the swirly anyway when Meander and Ecknoreial got together and decided to put an end to some of my comfort zone issues.

I quickly became comfortable enough with my route and was moving into the euphoria of world traveler when I noticed a blinking yellow light up in the distance. The terrain was moderately hilly and curvy so I assumed there was probably a small burg up ahead and that I would have to slow down. Silly fear that it is, I am still overly-conscious of driving over the speed limit. Speed just isn't my middle name.

I slowed my cruise control and pushed onward. After driving for probably ten minutes, I realized there was nothing even closely resembling a caution light. I asked if they had made me see the light and they said *"yes, look up ahead and to your right."* I got up the road a bit further and there was a police car hidden in the pine trees. As I said, I usually tend to follow the rules of the road but seeing the police car as significant indicates I am still having fear in those areas.

Now, how does this relate to the bleed-through of swirly and forward movement? First I was amazed by the magic and that kept me clouded with possibility, or more precisely said, amazed that there was some connection with some being that watched over me; hence, spirit. It helped to create a little high to begin a new patterning pathway for my issues with travelling in unknown areas for any distance, and truth be known, that reason is only the surface of the issues in question. It was more about climbing out of my rut to try new things, but after avoiding a traffic ticket for, *for what*??? Gray roots that grow too fast??? Paranoia; a free trip with every swirly. Anyways, everything else went well on the trip to my mother's.

Then came the drive home. I had about five hours of anxiety so intense that I wanted to pull over, just abandon my car and call a taxi. My emotional reactions to my surroundings made no sense at all. It was like being in a fight-or-flight pursuit with no end. I am from a plains area with flat corn fields in every direction. About half an hour after leaving my mother's, the roads became what I laughingly remembered being called 'tickle-billy hills.' The only thing was, there was no laughter in this journey; every ride up a hill caused so much anxiety I wanted to jump out of my skin. I was expecting to fall right off the end of the earth. I tried the good ole primal-scream-technique a couple times, but not being a particularly angry person, screaming took more energy than it was worth; it didn't help a bit. There was no way to relieve the anxiety. The unexplained dread was literally dripping from my pores. And to complicate matters, I had to keep talking to my thighs to keep them from cramping; a new development in driving out of my comfort zone. My travel progressed in that fashion and I noticed that I drove slower and slower with no apparent ability to speed up, so fortunately I somehow managed to be alone on the road most of that part of my trip. Thank God no one was behind me; they might have scared me right over the non-existent, never-ending cliff at the side of the road.

I didn't think I could possibly feel worse than I did when I came within half an hour of the Gerald Ford Highway in Grand Rapids. For some reason my anxiety took an epic turn for the worst. I prayed and cajoled and begged for some release of the unbearable panic attack. Nothing came in the way of relief so I pushed onward, all the while getting driving lessons from the invisible gang. They would talk to me about how to manage the tough spots and how to find the best lane and then get comfortable with knowing that I might be in someone's way. I was too anxious to keep up with the speed of the center lane but using the right lane was causing so much panic with the merging traffic that I couldn't function there either. We are talking post-traumatic stress disorder at this level of discomfort. There was some reassurance with their instruction but the physical discomfort was more intense than I could possibly explain to you, at least unless you've had your own mega-swirly.

I can't tell you how many clients I see that are experiencing this overwhelming anxiety and they are tying it to something in the past or something so off-handed that it's almost silly, something even as silly as an old sciatic nerve condition. This is the first and biggest clue that you are in a swirly and the underground realities are in full play. Once the client understands what is happening, they are ready to just slow down for a bit and let the alternate reality pass. Knowing that this feeling doesn't portend something dreadful is really helpful. For me, finally I got through the heavy traffic and found my comfort zone. After that, the anxiety subsided and I even pulled off the interstate and found a Starbucks to chill – decaf, of course.

"You required forward movement in your routine of life. The blinking yellow light symbolized the slowing up of your feeling of progress."

Oh darn, I should have known. They sent me forward into the unknown in a way that at first relaxed me and they even inserted a little high so I thought I was free of my driving fears. That little high they inserted gave me some smiley faced files to use with future experiences. There were too many frownie faces in my traveling portfolio. Then on the way home they subconsciously addressed some of the negativity in other issues that I am not privy to as of yet. This swirly resulted in one big sump pump clog. I was moving upward in vibration in that I could now even consider driving that far away and alone. I was also clearing the fears that kept me symbolically wanting to stay close to home, which amounts to staying close to the routine I knew well, i.e., staying in my usual patterns. The whole thing is this; my situation is symbolic of the fears that hold us in restrictive behavior patterns. The real areas being flushed during my self-diagnosed episode of PTSD are unknown to me but the emotional residue permeated my waking mind to the point that I came to associate it with driving in unknown areas. The truth of my traveling flush is far more complex and really had more to do with moving forward with my life without holding onto old patterns of comfort rather than embracing new possibilities, but because I was driving out of my comfort zone, I associated the panic attack with that situation – which, by the way, was also being addressed in the spirit-led driving lessons.

I am noticing these flushing incidents are really amped up during episodes of respite care. During the healing time it takes for medical procedures, mishaps and even a hearty case of the flu, the SWIRLY IN PROCESS signs lights up *and the down time is used by us up here to open a new doorway into your mind and dismantle the clogged fear that has prevented the forward movement required to raise your vibrations upward in love. This does not mean we are causing these mishaps but we do take advantage of the down time to clean your minds and at times the resultant stress of the procedure does cause your physical vehicles to take slightly longer to heal than under normal circumstances. In truth, we wish you would all feel comfortable in taking your time when your body tells you we are in here clearing more fear."*

When mass consciousness is moving upwards in motion, it doesn't mean we are moving faster but it does mean we are learning faster. The common misconception here is that moving up in vibration means moving faster or having never-ending physical stamina. Actually, moving up in vibration means moving peacefully and comfortably with a whole lot more possibility, since the veil that hides the unlimited potential of our conscious minds is lifted somewhat. Moving faster to accomplish more is exactly what we don't have to do. It becomes more about what would I like to do and what can I do for those around me rather than what else can I do to convince myself and everyone around me that I am special, or better said, that I matter?

It is that sense of urgency stemming from fears that are trying to escape the pull of the flush that propels us forward more quickly than we would normally want to go. I did it this morning. My first clue should have been obvious when I tried to call my husband and dialed first, my daughter, who was in a time zone three hours behind me and had flown half the night to get there. So much for her peaceful rest. Then I called my own cell, knowing full well I had accidently given my daughter my cell charger when I took her to the airport. I was trying to save my charge for her pickup so she could text me when the plane landed. Then yet another flat tire that I drove on too long to fix was my next clue – and with a husband out of town, of course. I was definitely out of synch. The stops and starts of the repatterning were well in play.

I had given myself a list of very do-able things that had to get done and once I moved through the first chore, that impending doom of not having the rest finished surfaced with a good dose of anxiety, exhaustion and nausea – that just under the surface nausea that you must ignore or it tosses your cookies for you. That is typical behavior when in the midst of a swirly and trying to catch up with a forced shift in resonance at the same time. You over-react and then you're too tired to care. This happens often because our swirlys, many times, will overlap. We can be dancing with the swirlys at the same time that we slow our roads for another dose of repatterning, which can account for a good deal of the slow dancing we're trying to break out of lately. No wonder we're tired.

With my car in the shop and having been given the signs of being in the midst of a mega-swirly, I have a reading this afternoon. If I follow the signs laid out for me, it might not be my best work. I have negotiated some cooperation with the guides that peek into the auric fields of those around me. They do cooperate when I work, even if I'm out of synch in other areas. Still, I wondered about this read; I knew it would go fine but what often happens during these times of shift is that the client will be happy with the information but I won't have a clue as to whether they are or not. The invisible gang will block my ability to know when I hit the bull's-eye so I miss my secret, self-acknowledged kudos at being good at my work. I will feel as though I am off my game when in fact, I am not.

This is a very common occurrence during a swirly and repattern session. We are learning to self-inspire, to go within to find our sense of self and what is right for each of us, so the plug may be pulled from our usual waves of self-glorification. If I am in the icy rinse cycle again, I may have no clue that I am getting or giving the right advice. The reason is because I should not require the approval of someone else to certify that I am doing my best job. I should know from within. Now that is unfair to some degree because I have to be able to read the client's feelings well enough to know what flavor to use in presenting the entrée. Still, I will persist in somehow muddling through – but that's the thing; I feel as though I am muddling through it; there is no natural flow – even though we get there…somehow. That is *my* personal out-of-synch-with-work aspect of being in the swirly flow.

I can't tell you how many clients, as well as family members, report feeling so off their game that they're sure they are about to be fired or dumped or in danger of losing whatever it is that keeps them feeling good about self. This process will cause an unsureness in us that says we're just fumbling around, feeling our way back to the path that had become so well worn. In truth, we are being pushed out of our comfortable path and forced to move over far enough to have to forge a new path. That is part of the slow dance of repatterning. What motivated us before will no longer fit. We will be pushed along with unexplained owies or other physical, mental and emotional uneasiness that keeps us from finding our former nest of comfort.

There are a couple reasons for this phenomenon, one being that we require a different venue for self-validation. We are sure we are doing well when someone else tells us so, but what if we were lacking in all human feedback for a week or two? We would begin to use a different sense of self-government. We would search for a higher integrity within. If our needs are not met by someone else, we will learn to meet them for ourselves. To do so requires an understanding of self in a way that completes self. After doing a few too many psychic fairs without feeling my normal elation at hitting the mark, I begin to ask – and ask again – how to fix this. More than once I decided that I was done teaching classes or done doing fairs because I felt so off my game. I would always be amazed when shortly after my decision to give it all up a client would return to tell me how helpful I had been.

That's the thing, we go through swirlys regularly to clean up our subconscious and let the light in to other possibilities, because at some point you will more than likely have to make an important decision during a flush. You might as well learn how to do it well now; it will save a lot of headaches, bounced checks and lost friends later.

I am coming out of this swirly with the idea that I am pushing through; it is time to accomplish some of the things I really want to do, which isn't all that much – write a book or two and drop some weight. I have played with the Most Wanted List long enough that I find I can manifest much of my simpler materialistic desires. As I have moved through these gyrations of aligning intentions and desires for the good of the group, I can honestly say that I am thankful for all I have and don't really want for anything that much. I am learning that what I really wish for comes through naturally. So now it is time to put some *push through* energy on those two things that stay constant in my desires, but because they feel overwhelming in scope I tend to relegate them to the back burner. Drop some weight; write the book.

I am too heavy, but five years ago I was even heavier. I didn't eat much, contrary to what you may be thinking, but I did eat a lot of smoke when it came to easing out of my comfort zone. I can honestly say that I didn't let my weight bother me like it might some because I had a weight problem by the time I was three years old. It is normal for me to be bigger than everyone around me. I don't see myself in that way most of the time. I can be the biggest person in the room, which has happened more times than not, but I no longer notice my size, for the most part. Somewhere deep inside me, I discovered that I liked me, and once I discarded the need to be physically desirable, I attained a freedom that allowed me to enjoy people for who they are instead of maneuvering around them based on whether or not they approved of sexual attractiveness or lack thereof.

I stem from very attractive parents whose focus tended to be on their physical attributes, so being the fat little kid was overly-noticed by them and consequently by me. My mother worried that I ate too much one day and the next day I would hear her tell the doctor that I didn't eat anything. I remember the doctor telling me to eat only one hamburger or one peanut butter sandwich instead of two. Playing my role of good little girl, I would nod and agree, knowing somehow I must have been at fault again. I really didn't know how to tell him that I already only ate one. Heck, where would I get another one? There were seven kids to feed.

In high school I managed to get my weight down to 120 pounds, but I could only eat one thing a day, plus I was on speed, a.k.a. diet pills, amphetamines, uppers; whatever you want to call them. They were all the rage and easily accessible. Normally I weighed 140 to 150 lbs., depending on my moods, and although closer to the average person now, still bigger at that time than most. My mother might have weighed 115 on her fat days – something I haven't seen since seven years old. To get her pills, she would put ball bearings in her coat pocket so she weighed heavier. If that didn't work, she would send me in. Surely they wouldn't deny the fat kid her speed.

I didn't like being on those pills; I didn't always make the best decisions when I felt so amped up. By nature I am easy going and at peace with most things. My mother called it lazy and maybe it was in a way, but for me there is more to life than trying to control my weight or chasing balls around on a court. I can diet, but the food intake had to be so low that I would wrestle with my rebellious sense of deprivation or become obsessed with eating because I had to make sure I didn't break the rules. I have made a lifetime career out of joining and quitting Weight Watchers. It is the ideal program for some but not for me. Since I was a kid, I ate primarily once a day. Weight Watchers taught me to eat three meals a day and then I had to become so overly conscious of my food and weight that I got bigger; I added another layer of fear to my fat. I have fasted with the local hospital – twice, and at no small expense, only to get bigger. When I say that I have spent thousands of dollars on diets and got bigger every time, I am not exaggerating. Suffice it to say, I can't afford to get any bigger so I gave up dieting. I am programmed to fail when it comes to diets – seriously. Rationalization that may be, but if I just forget about it, I do better – a lot better.

So I have made some progress by forgetting about it. I listen to my body as far as food but I am also trying to throw out the belief systems that do not work for me. I ask you, how can it be that one Oreo cookie has seventy calories and can be eaten in one bite if you're stressed, two if you're taking your time to play with the cookie and twist it apart, or three bites if you're trying to be dainty, but let's face it, there's no point in being dainty with an Oreo, they break too easy and get crumbs on your boobs – and still take half an hour walking to work off one serving. Exaggeration aside, it just doesn't make good sense to me. Somebody's belief system made that too hard.

If we create our own reality, then why can't my Oreos have ten calories or why can't I burn at least a hundred calories for every para-graph I type? The truth is, I am cerebral and not physically active but quite happy – do I have to change my normal way of being to keep my name off the *persons to avoid at all costs* charts that the insurance companies use? I really am pretty healthy. All the blood work comes out well enough and I have no complaints other than a slow-to-leave zit just under my left cheekbone. OK, the top of my foot hurts but at least I know why. I just don't want to spend $500 for a specialist to give me a shot of cortisone and I know my sore foot is swirly-related and keeps me asking myself if I am holding my thoughts up far enough, plus it is tied to a repatterning - but all shift related and will heal in time. ***As a side note, it is now six months later and the sore foot-top comes and goes. It usually surfaces when I am in a repatterning stage and trying to hold my mental constructs up higher than my raw emotional reactions are behaving. This is a normal part of the dance of repatterning; the emotional reactions take a little longer to shift than the mental perceptions. Think of it this way: when the top of your foot hurts, you might be banging it on the next ladder rung of awareness – you can't quite make it up the next step yet, but you're getting there.

Finally I am coming out of this swirly and I am realizing that these couple things that I really want are not changing and I am going to have to put some effort into making them happen because I can fill up my day with things that are so much easier to achieve, but at the end of the day, I still want to feel like a normal sized person and I still want to write about what I am learning with the invisible gang. And let's just say it now – both desires are products of my own fears, but if I have to go through this process, maybe I can help others by letting them know it's not the end, just a new beginning, or more honestly said, maybe I can feel better about myself by sticking with the projects that feel so overwhelming.

During this process I have dropped about forty pounds and at least twelve inches in my waist. That's probably not a normal weight loss pattern since other body parts didn't fluctuate as much but I am told by the invisible faction that they orchestrated the loss so that it came off where it would help me most discover myself again. Taking some of the tire out of my middle made movement a whole lot easier. The totally cool thing is, it happened simply by letting it go and by changing my belief systems about eating and food. I am not even close to where I want to be in either case yet, but I am making some slow headway. I have to release the guilt that comes with eating and I have to release the fear that I have incorporated into what I eat and I have to leave behind the old belief systems that tell me that I can't eat without doing my body harm in some way. Plus, I make an attempt to listen to my body and its needs, something I was actually doing better before the swirly process came into play. Seriously, I kind of lost that ability when I was learning to throw away the guilt, but I am working on reprogramming that one. The weird thing about this process is that there are times, especially during swirly and repatterning cycles when all my body will even consider without becoming nauseous is – dare I say it – desserts. What is that saying? Desserts spelled backwards equals Stressed – the big symptom of a swirly and the long-term goal in fear-flush, to alleviate unnecessary stress. If dessert is all you can handle, there is a very good chance your alternate-reality-dream-state is in full operation. Take a nap if you can sleep and if you can't, grab the corn chips and marathon a whole season of something you always wanted to watch but never had time.

The point is, in altering your belief system, you have to create a new one and I am determined to create a physical vehicle that doesn't require attention on food as a culprit and massive amounts of exercise to have a normal sized body. I am a cerebral being; my thoughts should be burning massive amounts of calories, and truth be known, we're all headed in that more cerebral direction. Maybe the calorie-belief-system should be flushed with that change in our mental evolution. Our belief systems should provide some correlation between a person's strengths and metabolic processes, and they do once we clear the restrictive format we've inadvertently set up for ourselves. Unfortunately, our belief systems have come to include nutritional requirements that cannot be met without eating, and calories of heat to count in such a way that it is damn near impossible to hold a physical body in check without blowing it in one direction or the other, unless you like living life like it is one big race. Too many of our beliefs stem from our fears. They are overly-prevention-oriented or they are attempts at correction that cause an over-focus on the non-desired end result. Metaphysics for Muggles 101 will tell you that what you resist will persist until you can shift your mental and emotional focuses to that desired end result.

As long as we're flushing the fear from our perceptions, now is the time to heal the old paradigms that no longer serve us effectively. We have created our perceptions of how things happen, how they work and how they should be, so it seems to me that if they're not working well anymore, once the fear is cleared we have the perfect time to create new and easier beliefs. It is the belief in something that makes it real. Believing it to be so is like adding a chemical catalyst to a mix of components to make them come together in a cohesive and perfectly blended end result. I know that we're not all dealing with weight issues but we are becoming so focused on what we can't eat and why we can't eat it that we are creating one very narrow path of acceptability in regards to nourishing our physical bodies. Plus, I am not convinced that food is always such a big part of additional weight; aspects worth looking at might be the emotional impulses that cause us to want to eat combined with our shame in looking or not looking certain ways. So what is required now is a better sense of understanding our personal motivations and tapping into the guidance within to help us solve and resolve the fear hiding in our emotional pantries.

So lately I have been slower moving than I want to be. I felt a pull towards the subconscious resolution of what keeps me from moving forward in the ways that I really want to propel myself. After these few weeks of plodding through my gelatinous life, all the while making the necessary steps in the usual directions, I had to face myself with a new realization; although happy with myself in many ways, these couple long range projects are more important to me than I have been able to admit to myself. Because they are so large in scope, I am afraid of losing momentum before I reach the end. I am tending to everything else first. Procrastinating? Perhaps and yes, but more I am recognizing that my desire has not changed in these areas and that the reasons for wanting to do them are of a higher vibration than before. So what is the missing piece in my puzzle of slow movement?

This morning I saw a vision of a horse, looking down at the ground and standing still. Having learned to see the horse as a symbolic representation of will, I instantly knew that I had to change the positioning of the horse. Mentally, I raised the horses head upward, to symbolize a change in scope of vision, and then I caused him, with my will, to move forward into a comfortable canter. I instinctively knew that in changing my vision of the slow and unmotivated horse, I was symbolically changing my pattern of movement in regards to the projects that still await my attention. The fact that the horse showed up at all in this vision was for me a confirmation that my prayers for help had not gone unnoticed, although results will still require my own personal efforts, hence the *will* aspect of the vision. That is a symbolic example of using the vision board of our minds in creating our reality. Our dreamscapes are clogged with the residue of unresolved fears but if we can tap into that dream light with our waking mind, we can take charge of those random thoughts and send the creative energy off in the direction of our desires. The vision was a subconscious representation of my desire to push forward in the large scale projects of my life. Both Ecknoreial and Meander were involved. Kind of keep that little vision-changing scenario in the back of your mind because later on, after the inbox of subconscious resolution begins to taper off, that is the beginning of re-solving the unresolved from our dream state – while awake - and using the visions to create your desired end results.

Something else became very clear during that peek into my wis-dom-aura; I haven't been listening to Ecknoreial about much of what runs through my mind, as I had hoped, but Meander. It is Meander that I need to reason with; it has been Meander giving me advice, and her level of reasoning is not quite up to par. Meander represents my sub-conscious reasoning and subconscious reasoning is very closely tied to our raw emotional reactions – our stimulus-response behavior. That's where all those ideas of reptilian aliens originate. A good deal of our dream activity is Meander trying to resolve the negatively-tainted en-ergy to a more love-based awareness. What I had failed to realize was that most of the time Meander was presenting me with my most instant feelings about things and because she was speaking so loudly in my mind, I was confusing her perceptions with the higher realm percep-tions of the Ecknoreial group.

Most resolving dream activity is an attempt to clear the errant emo-tional reactions to our world. Our mental perceptions are progressing well at times but it takes a while longer for the emotionally motivated Meander to catch up. We can better correct the immature emotional status with our conscious mind and we are learning to do so now be-cause our Ecknoreial groups are with us orchestrating our own personal swirly processes. We can't escape the thoughts running through our conscious awareness because they refuse to be turned off until we turn off the old, fear-tainted programming.

Meander's voice of reason is one of the more topical layers in guiding protection; the learned behaviors we instill within ourselves as true and correct. This includes our defenses as well as our wisdom-center. Now that Ecknoreial has become involved in the clean-up, she will direct our thoughts in ways designed to awaken our wisdom-centers to our immature feelings. Feelings CAN and should be changed to reflect a higher level of maturity. One big key in self-correction is this; just how self-centered am I in this scene? Self-love has more to do with being at peace with self than it does with proving to self that self is worthy.

To correct these layers of self-centered feelings, Ecknoreial initiates a line of thought that appears to repeatedly leap through your mind with no apparent connection to an off-switch. Once that mental-vision-loop refuses to stop, take your own feelings out of the equation and look at the whole scenario long enough to see why your feelings about it are in error. From there, practice the axioms of a love vibration:

*Do no harm,

*You are responsible for and can only change yourself,

*Everyone is right from their perspective at that point in time,

*Ideally, in a love-based reality, your feelings about everything should be feelings of peace.

Now apply those perceptions to said-situation until it begins to dissipate and you find it easier to change your focus to something else. Once you get the emotional reaction ironed out, your Ecknoreial group will stop running it through your conscious mind. Another point to keep in mind here is that this thought will usually stem from the past but there is more than likely another situation in your present that is of the same octave of reasoning. The past scenario is being used because of the similarity in feeling and pattern of immature reasoning that your mind is using to make peace with it. Using the past keeps us from re-energizing the discomforts of the present but once said logic is correct, visualize a garage door closing on the scene and re-close it every time it pops up.

When this particular training-pattern starts it indicates that an update in our emotional reactions is being downloaded for us so we can begin to pattern our feelings on a higher plane of maturity. The sticky wicket here is that I have to reason more with Meander because she is the special needs aspect of me that requires more input from me to be able to address things effectively. My own patterning is still holding me back and my heart-tied and feeling-centered Meander gets at least part of the credit. Meander can be described as an overly-used layer of subconscious reasoning where our raw emotional reactions are used to start our reasoning engine; a layer that must be matured so that our dream state can relax into a more productive cycle of creation.

Truthfully, that is how this process is working. You may not be hearing the voices in your head 24/7, but your subconscious mind is sending you the same kind of subliminal information, some of which is subterfuge that is often times masked as superconscious information straight from higher self. Ecknoreial can send messages into your thoughts, some coded to come up at a certain time and others as she sees the need, routed all through your subconscious. Plus, your subconscious is in there having coffee with the group of guide aspects helping Meander to clear the fear. They're sitting around the table with their coffee and orange-cranberry scones, watching you all hooked up to a virtual reality system, living out the custom-alternate-reality designed to clear some fear-based distortion in your perceptions. The thing they don't tell you is that in order to clear the fear, some of the alternate realities you experience underground are much worse than what is already programmed in your present reality package. So as the experience plays out on the console in front of your subconscious, you are consciously feeling the emotional residue that arises from said scenario. This intense emotion is allowed and encouraged to waft forth into your conscious awareness; hence, you now encounter anxiety in the form of PacMan of the Mean Head eating his way towards your correlating chakra areas. PTSD! Here we come...

Again, this intense emotion is stressful on your physical body and accounts for most of the owies and emotional discomfort you hold when there is no other apparent reason. I have to wonder if we're not confounding our health care professionals with swarms of stress-related maladies with no apparent cause. Of course I also have to realize that I see them as stress-related maladies because of my unusual experience with spirit and sorting through our love vibrations; they are having their medically-based-perceptional conclusions. Either way, Ecknoreial and Meander are in synch and out of synch during this process and will both work to slow you down and nudge you forward at the same time.

I am finally coming out of one of these little ditties and I had forgotten some of the discomforts and confounding little tricks. I had to check in with the voice that accompanies me now to ask how long it has been and she said at least a year and a half since I've had one like this. Last week I was feeling the strong urge to visit a shop that hosts some of my services. The urge was so strong that I left like a woman on a mission from god. This kind of stupid confusion is typical during this process but as I pulled out of the garage I noticed some working of the car much louder than usual but I couldn't figure out what it was. I started down the road and was in amazement as to how loud the normal sounds of the car were. Is something wrong? Did my hearing change in this process? Now don't laugh, because that is one of the typical tactics spirit (Ecknoreial) uses during these episodes; they make you hyper-aware of certain noises. A simple noise like the water-line in the refrigerator can be used to convince you that there is a bogyman standing right behind you. Just yesterday I had backed out of the drive and put the car in low instead of drive but fortunately I noticed the noise differential right away and was able to correct my mistake before I actually drove far enough to get out of low gear.

So this time I checked my pernandle to make sure I was in the right gear and kept going. The car felt sluggish and just not normal but I couldn't put my finger on it. After about a mile I knew I had to get out and check things; I just couldn't get comfortable with my new level of hearing car noises. Lo and behold, not only was my tire flat but off the rim. Crap! And then, toss common sense to the wind, I decided to drive it back home. When I think about this I can't quite believe that my mind was still operating my body but finally I limped slowly onto a side street of nothing but fields and tumbleweeds. I got just far enough into the road to nowhere when I knew I couldn't take the car further without doing real damage so I stopped and stared at the deserted terrain and asked for magic.

"Push Through..."

Gee thanks. I really could have used one of the fire place tricks at about that time and even reminded them that it would work well in the book, but no dice. So I did what every other mere mortal would have to do, call for help. Besides the embarrassment and the cost of two new tires, things turned out well but that is the sixth flat tire I have had since this process began. My husband makes little innuendos about me and tires now but I would bet money on it that the invisible faction has something to do with those flat tires.

"We do. You know it and he does not."

They have always happened during a swirly and have thus far resulted in six new tires for a car that is not yet six years old. I have learned that guide-speak will re-route the energy overflow so that it doesn't all manifest as physical symptoms. Have you had those weeks when the water heater goes down, then the dryer and then the toilet goes on a clog cycle? Well, consider this; you might just be saving your efforts for repatterning so they are sparing your achy-breakie heart any more abuse. In my case, there was a pattern of forward movement that is still in need of change.

"Push Through..."

That's the one. The slightest distraction can throw me off my bigger desires because I am afraid of not finishing them, which in my mind still equates to putting all that work into it only to fail. What's the worst that can happen? This is how I deal with it; it works, but it shouldn't. I have never been able to simply lose the weight. I am already living with that and it doesn't hurt. I just have hopes of buying smaller clothes and more agility. I could finish a book that no one wants; it happens all the time. This isn't the first book I started or finished. If I couldn't sell it could I do another or just give up?

Acutely aware of that possibility keeps me wanting to do a better than perfect job of it and I can't get to that point while I am still inside my head. I have to take the chance that you and I can find enough harmony that my story makes sense to you. It's a risk, and a big one, but I can do it. I just have to plan time into my day to sit here even if I erase everything I write and start over, but even that has already happened many times, so what's my hold-up now? Surely I can do this.

The symbology of those flat tires bears explaining. Often times in our symbolic universe, your car may represent your physical vehicle – the body. I am, of course, speaking of the symbology that is used while we're in our dream states. Since my tires are responsible for moving me around, a flat tire would represent my lack of will, energy and desire to move forward in some area. Fixing and replacing the tires are indicative of my need to push through in some new way. It's like saying, once again you ran out of steam before you got where you wanted to go.

That is a confusing statement because during the fear flush, higher self will help you run out of steam just to slow you up and then Meander will indicate that you're slacking again. The crux of this is that it is Meander's pattern we are trying to break; i.e., what feeling is off in all of this? It will be necessary to take those feelings up in maturity before we get much help in moving forward. Just so you know, at some point we rescue ourselves in all of this. Use your own discernment as to when and where you are going, but when my tire's flat again, I can almost be sure I'm missing the mark on some particular pattern that is in need of realignment. I do not mean to imply that this is the case for every flat tire for everybody on the planet. It is *my* sign right now and six flat tires is a strong indication that somebody invisible might be messing with the inner pressures of my forward movement – that is fear flush in operation. You get to know your own individual signs. And before you ask, yes; we've had the car checked for defects.

Why would dream state symbology apply to your waking life? Well, that's just it, your dream state is one of the creative sides of your conscious mind once you clear the fear. There is a direct correlation between the alternate realities playing out down under and some of the mishaps up here on the main floor. That is exactly what I mean about the energy over-flow being rerouted so you can keep your feet and hands in useable condition. All those sore thumbs, heels and toes out there? Now you're getting it…the top of my foot was already hurting; the flat tire hurt less.

One more thing that it might help to understand: in the midst of the fear flush, some atypical reinforcements are used to help curtail undesirable thought patterns. I call it the creep-out factor. You may have noticed lately that you will hear a lot about spirit activity with anyone and everyone who has an interest in such things. Our invisible factions are making themselves known and in ways that aren't always offering peace, tranquility and love. For the purpose of the creep-out, they show up when you're thinking in the wrong way or when your ideas are just not all that high in vibration.

A few years ago my son was working the dinner shift at a local college. I would drop him off at work and come back home for a couple hours of quiet time. Just as I would settle into whatever I was going to do, the area above me – which was his bathroom, would deliver one big crash – like someone picked up the toilet and dropped it on the floor. " *It's us* " was all they would say. There was no mistaking that something was out of sorts somewhere. Finally, one night my husband happened to be home with me when it happened. We both sat there and looked at each other until he finally said, "I'm not going up there…ask your Gs what that was."

"It's us."

We both had the experience of the mysterious raining commodes a couple more times and then my physical discomforts and stiff, achy lower body appeared to lighten up. My mind relaxed and I actually rediscovered a quietness in there so that I could even meditate again. I knew I had reached a higher stair finally and could breathe easier and move forward without the mishaps and exhaustion. There really was no wayward entity attaching to us or our house but more a case of Ecknoreial and the behaviorist techniques she used to keep me from returning to an old way of dealing, feeling, rehearsing or purging.

Now before I scare any of you who have not experienced some of these more intense scenarios, let me just say a couple things. First, every noticeable episode of spirit activity is not a prophesy of impending doom. It usually serves to alert you that your thoughts, words or actions are going down the drain in regards to that love vibration I keep talking about. I'll just bet that the falling toilets were timed to match my own drop in emotional-feel-good-energy because I knew my rest was only temporary; I still had the other half of my chauffeur duties awaiting me and at a point in the day when I was beginning to tire. For me, getting tired is an invitation to change my inner channel to the supercilious blues. My next point is that everyone of sound mind is flushing their fears but not everyone is able to be pulled out of the mainstream to handle the more intense incidents. My husband seems to have a more constant but gentle swirly, but he is working and travels and has to be up and about and clear-headed. I, on the other hand, have the luxury of being able to fall on my snoot and then lie around and nurse my wounds. So if you're life requires that you be up and moving, you will be. There are some who will never know they are flushing their anger or quietude but they will go through the same process and achieve the same results, just with a less intense format.

If you are experiencing these unwelcome visits from the invisible factions of your life, let me just explain how this works so you don't have to fear them. If you're interested in spirit-based phenomena, they will use these tactics to get your attention in a way that reinforces your belief in spirit activity. Be it ghost-busting or angelic nose wiping, you know without a doubt there is something in there with you. Here's the important part though, your higher self is in charge of your auric field and will allow no one in there that shouldn't be. For the most part, at this dimensional vibration, that means no one else is in your auric field except you and your own private invisible faction. Your Ecknoreial knows best what you need and maintains perfect balance in that area.

The other thing is this: spirit is a love-based dimension and there are no bogeymen there. Think about it, the fear is here in the physical dimension. It stems from our fear of survival, of not being connected to something with more possibility than we have here and now, but once we cross back over, we lose that feeling-frequency. As soon as you leave the physical plane, you encounter the higher vibration and that takes you back to peace and harmony, back to your complete self, your immortality. It is our subconscious that holds that lower vibration and creates snarling little bears. Thank god its creative potential is quarantined.

"Some will say you are wrong here and we will address this in another book."

Why did you say that? It makes me think I am in error somehow and yet you have made sure I have an understanding of the love that exists just outside this vibration of mass consciousness and also that there really isn't a lower vibration than this, except for our subconscious, because of all the unresolved fear stored there. Even if there were a lower vibration out there beyond ourselves, because of the law of resonance – like energy attracts like energy...

"We are saying that you are not the one in error."

It's not time yet?

"No it's not; that's all."

"Now, does all energy achieve consciousness? Yes."

How?

"Once the energy spark is in use, the movement causes it to sense self. From there the options are unlimited."

Cool!

PS – Did you notice how they distracted me? And how I had to talk Meander through my fear of being misunderstood?

Swirlys have now become a normal part of our day-to-day existence and recognizing their nuances and subtle discomforts can actually help you to take further conscious control of your mindset and consequent life results. Working with the flow of the repatterning will bring the big easy button of manifestation into play sooner than if you just float around in a boat of confusion without considering that there may be a set of oars tucked just under the seats.

CHAPTER 7

WHAT HAPPENED TO MY PAST LIVES?

It's snowing again. I thought winter was over. My car skated across the ice as I chauffeured Brian to work and wondered again about the Mayan Prophesies. Based on some of the dogma I have come to accept as probable; is our earth really heading for a cycle of un-inhabitability or am I just tired of driving on slippery roads?

I don't really know what the end of the Mayan calendar signified but for me it has initiated a lot of thought provoking questions. In my mind, prophesy simply means possibility rather than a predestination, but what I really wonder about is the premise of the prophesy; why did the Mayans bring up this time period in the first place? Assuming at least part of it pertains to consciousness, that topic is still a vast and unknown territory while we're housed in our physical bodies. How far can we go while we're here and why do we do what we do in terms of incarnating into the slower realms – the physical – the waves of resonance that hold the fear? As soul sparks of consciousness, what did we hope to gain by planting a seed of self into the fecund fields of physical possibility? Was it really *this* place, sparked with splashes of negativity too broad in scope to rise above of our own volition that called to us with its siren song? Not to sound defeatist but here we are requiring divine intercession to pull ourselves out of a quagmire of tainted emotional reactions. If the planet is truly preparing to take a bit of down time, will we continue this experiment here or somewhere else, or will we fly as far as possible from planets with the capability of physical life and hope never to encounter such circumstances again?

I wish I could just ask these questions and instantly hear the right answers. Instead, when I ponder such vast existential concepts, I first get the lessons I need to understand the answer in terms of myself and why I might be asking in the first place. Then, if I'm still asking, the answers might come along to something more cosmic than just plain 'ole me trying to hold a love vibration. I have been questioning the whole of possibility and the differences between the spirit world and physical realm for some time, but this morning as I drove through another lingering blast of winter, something akin to an understanding began to form in my mind. Guide-speak would supply the necessary comments while I rambled through the concepts and watched as the puzzle pieces began to swim into the forefront of my consciousness, seemingly on their own. I knew they were being supplied by a higher power but they came to me as part of my own mental awareness, rather than a separate voice. Once again, point worth noting: that is the usual way for higher self to send answers, at least until our vibration of mass consciousness rises a few more degrees on the love meter so that the crown chakra opens enough that we can literally hear those who guide us.

My thoughts stemmed from one of the currently held ideas that we are coming to a certain point in the earth's patterns of cyclic travels where the planet experiences some harsh weather conditions. For those of us who aren't physicists, there is more involved in her movement and alignment than just the elliptical rotation around our sun. So, as I understand it now, this 2012-ish point in time and space is where our galactic council (i.e., baby-sitters for earth and her inhabitants) decided to initiate Operation Clean-Up for the vibration of mass consciousness, just in case we, the mere physical specimen, had been unable to bring it up on our own. A couple puzzle pieces that found their way to my understanding were that this time was chosen because earth has already begun her in-breath movement back towards the sun. In this case, the Mayan Prophesies were passed along as a result of a delay in this planetary movement. This may not be possible to understand but if you consider that our solar system is tied to a breath-type movement, as is all living creation, moving back towards the sun on an in-breath makes some sense. It might even account for some or even all of our global warming, among other things, but that is just a thought, not an actual piece of the puzzle. The next puzzle piece came in the form of guide-speak when they told me that our elliptical rotation of the sun was not ideal and required a re-formatting so that the rotation became circular again. I am not sure of this yet but it may be that our entire solar system requires an adjustment. There is more to it but at least now I kind of understand why this is the time for our divine intercession to raise the vibration of mass consciousness.

Now I am wondering, what happens several hundred years down the road, once a good deal of the negativity has been resolved? Will the planet ice over again and we wait in our spirit format for another chance to exist and evolve from the restricted realms? As I thought about that possibility I began to understand that we might have reached a stage of development, if our vibration of mass consciousness hadn't slipped, where we could have taken the helm as our own galactic councils with the capability of offsetting some troubling weather patterns while here in the physical. Is that what we're aiming for here? Do we keep working at this physical incarnation thing until we can handle pure creative energy while rooted here in the physical dimension? Handle it well enough that we actually manifest our physical reality? But alack alas, can't you just see a member of our galactic council using tactics as childish as a filibuster? I guess we're just not getting there on our own. Well, that's my point, maybe we could have been able to blow on that candle and light the wick, but we're still too in need of self-development to a point that self no longer matters as the number one consideration.

All of this thinking prodded me to ask; I am assuming we have all been doing this physical incarnation thing for quite a while, here and on other planets…???

With the healing of the vibration of mass consciousness at critical juncture, every possible wave of possibility is used to help us complete our understandings to the point that we never return to the old fear-based wave of negative programming or reasoning. The results of these complete understandings reaching critical mass, meaning for almost all of us, is that the entire wave of fear-carrying energy (that which we have risen above) will cease to exist, as will all past history stemming from the convoluted energy wave. It is for this reason that all possible techniques are being used to help us erase our past of discord and to learn all areas of study to the point that our awareness is complete. The erasure of conflict per se is our goal here and now. Once we achieve that higher wave of *cooperation for the good of the whole*, we can open doorways to higher waves of mental and physical possibility. All past history and tendency towards conflict will have been resolved and erased from our Akashic recordings.

Although I have changed in the way I see the magic of what lies beyond this realm, writing this book is probably the safest way for me to express my truth without taking exception to the beliefs of someone else; I used to struggle with judging what is different from my perceptive window, but I am getting better at accepting the stance that everyone is right for their individual circumstances. Our own unique viewpoints are used by our soul guidance to find our highest good. No one has to see it my way to find the answers; higher self will work with whatever window we look through to help us find our complete understandings. You don't have to be on a spiritual journey to become one with good/god. My philosophical platform may be different but that doesn't make all the others invalid, just not mine at this moment in time. I tend to avoid religion in my life as it isn't the perfect format for my perceptions, but I have a brother who is religious by nature and quite devout. He inspires me with his devotion to the good of all. Our perceptive windows are different and yet our basic philosophies and the lessons we are attracted to at certain times are very similar, even identical in concept and conclusion. I have another brother who dedicates his life to having a good time; a beer and the winning ticket are the perfect condiments for life, and he wants no part of religious doctrine or even of the idea of a god. He will tell you that if god existed he would never allow the suffering of this world to persist. His perceptive window is across the hall from some of the more religious factions, but I can tell you this; he gets the same lessons and arrives at the same conclusions as the religious window and the metaphysical window. It doesn't matter how you see the world or what indoctrination you employ, there is a deeper level of conceptualization out there and with the flush of fear, we are better able to recognize the similarities in our mindsets and to discover that *right* – our true north – will line up perfectly in the end.

When I first started working with spirit guides, what floored me the most was that I had guides of my own. I really didn't know that. I knew they were out there but thought they kinda' floated around and dropped in on whoever was a good girl that day or who really needed more help than me. Somehow I felt as though I had to do something big to get their attention and knowing they were speaking to me, even through someone else, was big because I felt as though I had finally been noticed by a spirit being. In all transparent honesty, it helped me feel better about me.

Now comes the fear-flushing subconscious realignment and resulting dimensional shift. We're beginning to understand finally that we all have a guiding higher self and that we are never without direct attachment to something bigger in awareness than us. The channeling that fascinates us is designed to provide us with that knowledge. There is something bigger out there and it is speaking privately to each of us even though we can't always discern what it is being said, hence the voice from nowhere calling your name every now and then or the unexplainable radio stations with songs or voices just out of your reach. Just climb one more stair in emotional maturity; you're about to hear the music of the spheres; the voices of the crown chakra.

We're at that point where many of us know we are connected to a higher source than just plain ole us; we're ready to move on in our understandings of how this really works because we really are at the aperture of the pyramid and ready to create our own reality. The next step in the dimensional shift is to lose our attachment to the fascination with our ability to connect to our own higher source and to use it as a browser for life and life's solutions. This will require a period of losing interest in what the channels and the invisible factions have to say long enough to realize we are getting it without the prove-it-to-me voice of external confirmation. Once we develop the security that we are getting the input we need from the higher realms, we can dispense with the paradigms designed to convince us there is an invisible world around us and we can begin to learn to create our own magic. This will also require some further understanding of how energy really works, especially between us and the spirit realm.

Back when I was young and impressionable, back even before I started searching for myself in history's trash can, I had always known, or at least suspected that I had lived during WWII and that I had been in the German military. My inner suspicions wafted between being male and female, a curiosity in itself, but later in life a series of dreams led me to believe that I had been a German male with one boot in the French resistance. But then as I shared that information with those of like belief systems, I realized I had nothing unique there; many of us believed we had been involved in WWII and then hurried back this time to finish some elusive mission. I know, supercilious eyebrow again.

I should have known something was amiss but then the search for signs and long-lost spirit friends kept me feeling involved and part of something bigger. I know now something was missing in me. A lot of people died in WWII and there may well have been an influx of souls wishing to finish off certain aspects of understanding, but for me, I am beginning to realize that I, personally, am too clouded with the fears of my here and now to have need of the information from my soul's past history, let alone access to it.

I believe in reincarnation, yes, but I have come to view it a little differently now than before my dance with spiritual vertigo. And I have to tell you that it feels right this time; I might be wrong but I do think that even if I am off course there are probably still some missing pieces of the puzzle, at least as far as the soul's journey, which just might come to light now, in this epoch of transformation. We are ready to learn more. We are bridging the gap to other aspects of consciousness so maybe it is time for us to recognize that we are not alone; there is a higher power attached to us at all times, but even better, that we are becoming capable of doing it on our own; taking conscious control of our life-reins.

Way back in my first world history class, sixth grade to be exact, I had my initial contact with the Holocaust and WWII. Always interested in certain time periods and in historical context in general, I was easily inspired to the further study of certain events. But this time my reaction was new to me; I became hyper-aware of a side of myself that was in a state of shocked disbelief that such atrocities could take place. The idea that WWII was a part of our very recent history had something to do with what bothered me. Attila the Hun and Caligula were different; the history was so long ago that it was beyond my realm of comprehension, but WWII included my parents and grandparents, real people.

Guide-speak tells me that was the trigger for me; my own disbelief that normal, thinking and feeling human beings could behave in such a way, but I feel that way about war in general so I accepted their input as having some degree of resolution in my pseudo-brush with Adolph Hitler's regime. However, that intense emotional reaction held my interest in that time period until I began to process portions of my own life from that perceptive window. This phenomenon resulted in a series of dreams, daydreams and unfounded suspicions that were always substantiated if I searched hard enough.

It was my high emotional reaction and my intense desire to know more of the time that made me realize that I was perhaps part of the original character cast. Once that thought took conscious form within me, way back in the early 70's, I toyed with the idea and then finally decided to let the memories flow. I slowed my conscious mind with a meditative state and then asked to remember the life that always felt just on the periphery of my awareness.

First I was aware of a cool breeze licking my face and the echo of my clicking boots as I walked down a brick street lined with dark shop fronts. I felt, rather than saw, the curious glances from the hidden faces behind the windows and doors and I just knew that there was a type of curfew in place that kept the secret onlookers from stepping out into the open. I noticed the quiet reflection of the occasional street light as I passed puddles of water from a recent downpour. I was acutely aware of my thoughts and knew that as I walked, I wrestled with a concept bigger than I wanted to tackle. I remember the thought, "I have the power to leave here but my conscience will not allow me to take the easy way out."

That little flash of memory, or more likely, that subconscious-created vision, that symbolic layering of my unresolved ploys in life, imprinted my mind well enough that I never lost the panorama or the accompanying feelings of not fitting in, of being alone in my perceptions. It happened just like the books said it would; all my senses were involved and alive and the emotion was turned on high. I felt so trapped and yet not trapped if I found the courage to step outside…..maybe outside of myself???

Not long after that, and just so you know how guide-speak works, I had occasion to witness a channeler. We're still talking the late 70s or early 80s here; channeling was just coming out of the closet and Ramtha was beginning to make a big splash. Jubal, another entity coming through about that time came along for me just as I began to wish for the chance to observe this amazing spectacle. I was particularly quiet in new situations and although I was thrilled to be asked to this private gathering, I was uncomfortable in not knowing many in the audience and feeling slightly out of synch with the group around me. Some I had encountered before but I had already established a pattern of *quiet Rhonda* with them and once that pattern is in place, it can be hard to break out of the mold. So I sat silently, willing Jubal to notice me and answer my big, secret question without my having to ask it.

Of course Jubal's discourse was on love; what else? I was already familiar with this thing called unconditional love and was even putting great effort into trying to reach that state when I wasn't too tired or too distracted. At the end, Jubal allowed some questions from the audience. Oh how I wanted to ask about that past life but oh how I didn't want anyone to know that I needed attention, so instead I sat, praying as loudly as I could in the language of silence – please, please notice me.

Well, he did. He answered some questions and finally turned to look directly at me and when I made no move to ask, he nodded his head as though he had heard my inner pleas. Still too self-conscious to just put it out there, I prefaced my question with my usual subterfuge, telling him that I knew it was not all that important but sometimes I wondered about my past lives because at times I was sure I still felt them. He took some time to explain that I carried with me some very recent pain from a life cut short in WWII. Of course I saw emotional fireworks and shooting stars for a few seconds while I assimilated that I had been correct, such was my joy of confirmation. My mind began to jump with all kinds of trampolining thoughts and for a brief time I lost my focus on what he was saying, but I will never forget one line of his explanation because, in true guide-speak, it was a riddle. Beware of those riddles, they usually mean you're barking up the wrong tree but they are giving it to you in the language you can best relate to at that moment in time.

He said, *"you died under the guise of a German official."* Well what the heck was the guise of a German official? Does that mean that I was a disguised German official or that I was killed by one? If you try to dissect that riddle, the possibilities are many and varied, but needless to say he provided a framework for my suspicions to take on an even more real tone. After that, in my dreams I would often take the form of a German male of some branch of the Nazi military, who lived in terror. In one dream I listened as a guide explained to me what happened to Eric, as I had come to *know* my name to have been then, so sure was I of this being a part of my past-life web of memories.

Years later, I was going through a particularly rough time on the job where my influence up until the coming of a new manager had been well-respected, but with the change in leadership I was no longer a voice to be heard. About that time, I had a dream of a dismal POW scene with a dour sense of confinement. The invisible voice explained that they had killed Eric by coming up from behind him to cut his throat, which, by the way, is information Ecknoreial would stay clear of and a good clue that I was looking at Meander's attempts to resolve something in my present. Superconscious awareness is an octave or three above the wave of resonance that includes murder. At the end of the dream, I remember hearing, "They buried his body in the stalag with the prisoners, where no one would think to look for him."

"We took that from your subconscious memory of Hogan's Hero's."

Right; Stalag Thirteen. No need to bore you with the symbology there; I know you get it, but wait; there's more! At one point, I was reading an old biography on Hitler and the author mentioned that Hitler believed there was one certain day in the year that held great power for him. I instantly knew that day was my birthday and lo and behold, I turned the page to find out that was exactly right. Now how did I know that and why *my* birthday in this life? Please, don't even begin to look at the pathetic symbology in that one...supercilious eyebrows abound.

"We knew; you didn't. It kept you searching for self in a way that took the sting out of things."

Well 'ouch' anyway. So in another dream I was a male with very tired, sore feet and had just come home after a long hard day. I sat down on the couch and pulled off my dirty boots when there came a loud pounding on the door. Most significant in the dream for me was the terror I felt when I heard the knock on the door. I opened the door to see two men in official uniform, one asking me to step outside, please. I almost fainted; I knew this was it; I was about to be found out. Found out about what I have no idea but the dread was so intense that I could hardly breathe. I realized that they were men that I worked with, and hoping to stall them while I figured out what to do, I said to them that I had just pulled off my boots and was done for the day when they laughed and said, "We don't care how bad your feet smell, get out here so we can talk."

Realizing that the visit was friendly and not in an official capacity, I stepped outside only to wake up shivering in fear. I don't remember the exact circumstances of my life at that time but I do know that at that stage I was still overly afraid of anger and had a hard time processing someone else's bad moods in that I did experience emotional reactions of being in danger and I still reacted as though I was the cause of said anger.

"That was it. You were always afraid someone didn't want you to talk to them because their indifference indicated to you that you were already rejected."

Translation: what I perceived as indifference had somehow become entangled with my fear of anger. Complicated but that's why it isn't easy to sort out our subconscious residue without the help of a swirly or two. I can keep going with all my dreams and faux-memories of life as a Nazi double agent (tee he) but how about I spare you and get on with how it all works?

First of all, like in a psychic reading, Jubal was able to read my auric field and pull out of my conscious and subconscious minds the questions and past references to my double life in Hitler's regime. Jubal was *"in all surety,"* a member of the soul family for Jerry Prim, the channeler. As already mentioned, at this vibratory rate of mass consciousness, it is necessary for higher self to act as buffer and translator when visiting the auric field of another. Jubal gave me just the confirmation I wanted without my having direct access to the Akasha. An interesting point worth noting here is that guide-speak tells me that it usually takes about two hundred years to get another stint in the physical realm. We have to wait on the baby production line, and quite frankly, they are hoping we slow that factory down.

Second, reincarnation is not understood as well as it could be. We have risen on our elevators of perception now and we can have some new pieces of the puzzle if we can shave off our old patterns just enough to allow the format to come together in a more group oriented and less personal way. Simply put, we just weren't ready to hear about it until our sense of self became more complete. With the clearing of the fear comes a point where we don't have to paint grandiose pictures of ourselves in our past lives because we can appreciate the here and now. We don't have to put our relationship woes into a past-life perspective so as to allow us to avoid our real responsibilities in regards to those around us. We are responsible for ourselves, and in a true love vibration we will have no expectations from others. All that means is we come from our highest and best good with self and that we recognize the beauty and truth in every single being out there; even good ole' Adolph Hitler.

I am a *retired* past life regression therapist and have had plenty of experience in helping clients move into a relaxed state of mind where higher self and the guide-aspects of choice can amaze and astound them. The guide aspects of choice will include Meander, and oftentimes, if the truth be known, Meander is the star of the show, at least at this vibratory rate of mass consciousness. She can pass along snippets of information geared to take the focus to a different place and time simply by pulling areas of interest out of current life files and applying them to whatever issues the client is chewing on in the recesses of all that unresolved business. Heck, that's what she does anyway as her full time job. I am actually pretty good at hypnosis and even use the relaxation techniques with clients when they are too anxiety-ridden to get much out of a reading. A well-modulated voice can do wonders in relaxing the inner turmoil. The process of relaxing the conscious mind when in an over-wrought condition serves to still the inner angst long enough to hear what is being said in a more comprehensive way.

As far as outcomes, I have never had a case where someone left with no results but I did have one occasion where I was left speechless when a woman who was having some trouble making any connections suddenly opened her eyes and said, "all I can remember is being a mermaid!" Well, alrighty then; they sure didn't cover that in past life school and at that point in my experience I didn't quite have the tools to decode it as I would now. First, I had doubts about regressing the client in the first place because she was wired and unable to quell her nervous energy long enough to focus on what she wanted to accomplish other than seeking some magic. Really it's the magic that we're after, but in this case, the excessive energy overload should have clued me in that regression wasn't the best route to take. It's like opening Meander's secret doorway to the conscious mind where she can allay the client's fears with a cartoon to keep said client occupied while she sifts through the debris. And rest assured there is no danger there; Ecknoreial will supply the symbolic cartoon so you won't have to suffer. Suffice it to say that the mermaid incident became my measuring stick for future decisions as to when to regress and when to quiet the angst with a consultation.

As I have come to understand this process during the tour of my intuitive self, I could have easily interpreted the results of this regression immediately. It goes something like this: In an attempt to reach our Akashic records, where all past life information is stored, we use a light hypnotic state to relax the subject and then lead them to the magic connecting point where they can tap into whatever information or memory their higher self provides. In fact, even though originally I didn't understand the meaning of higher self as well as I do now, I would give the directive that the subject have *higher self* take them where they most needed to go NOW. In retrospect, I can see that is exactly what would happen. They were actually at a point, since their conscious minds had relaxed a great deal, of allowing Meander to come out of the closet and attempt resolution to whatever pots were the closest to boiling over on the back burners of the basement kitchen. That is normal and exactly what happens when your mind tries to rest. I just helped you rest your mind and invited Meander out for tea. Frankly, and not to be crass, that's why so much mental work happens while you're in the bathroom. Our over-worked subconscious is seeking quiet time to come out and clean the kitchen and if we can just let our thoughts wander for a few, we might come up with a solution or a healthier outlook. But even perusing an outdated magazine will just keep adding more mental work, as our sub-conscious sees it. You'll know this to be true when you start fighting with the ads in your bathroom periodicals. So as I quiet the client's mind for a trip to the Akasha, poor Meander sees that opening door as a possible time to resolve the simmering pots on the front-most burner.

Pretend now that we have relaxed that conscious mind enough that Meander peeks out of the basement and asks what to work on first? So the alpha-state/dream-state kicks in and begins it resolution process. This is true with everyone and can be used well as a description of the workings of a past life regression since the intention to move into the past will always incorporate some element of fear in the desire; hence, a need to resolve. Oftentimes Meander's assessment as to what to resolve next is the exact situation symbolically referred to in the magical results of the regression. Whatever unhealed scenario is calling up from the basement of your mind the loudest will weave its way into the dream-like material and with the suggestive reasoning of the therapist, it can be talked through in a way that provides some degree of resolution for the client. Both Meander and Ecknoreial, along with the interests of the client, would be involved in providing the time-period cloaking of the scene so that the magical high would accompany the experience. It is possible and even very probable that similar instances from one's past lives would peek around the corner during this process to provide a glimmer of actual past life memory. I don't mean to dispute anyone's results or findings, I am just trying to bring our focus up to the here and now where we are transcending our ties to the past in order to move forward.

A past life regression works well in providing the client with a sense of being connected to something greater than self. It also helps the client to see things from a more productive perspective, as well as adding a little high to assist in raising the wave of resonance. In the case of the mermaid, I would have known by her obviously fragile state that she was far too emotional at that point in time to relax to a point of receptivity. She clearly needed to purge her fight or flight mentality before we could progress to a regression. The symbology was as clear as day; water is emotion and she was a mermaid; existing in pure emotion at that moment in time. I should have let her swim away for another day, at least until she could incorporate the symbolic land of reasoning into her outlook, but nothing was lost; she enjoyed stumping me with the mermaid memory. It was just the drama she needed.

There is a theory that a long and drawn-out relaxing process at the beginning of a regression serves to take the client past the subconscious and into the superconscious realm so as to get authentic material from the client's personal Akasha. That is great in theory, and would work in a higher vibration of mass consciousness, but since Meander has been relegated to the unconscious part of our conscious mind, she is really trying to step out more than we realize. In divine design, she was not meant to hide in the basement; she was part of a design team used to create our life circumstances. She was relegated to the basement when our vibration of mass consciousness became low enough that we could not resolve the fear in our outlooks without losing too much physical, mental and emotional energy. At that point, our galactic mentors took higher selves aside and instructed them to keep a more watchful eye on the kids playing down under and to hold off on letting us loose with our pure, creative ability, which is where Meander wishes to be more involved. Just like the rest of us in the work-force during tough times, she geared up for one job and can't quite get the promotion because there is no room at the top. At this point, Ecknoreial has asked Meander to take a guiding role and to hang in the basement and help clean up enough of the waste so that she can come back up and help with the design stage of the dreamscape when it is safe to resume such operations. This scenario is where we began to require sleep to process the negativity in our world. But now Meander wants her old job back and she is tired of working overtime to clear the way. The recession she experiences actually takes on mild symptoms of depression as she works overtime to get her special needs client back on task.

Since superconscious mind is not understood as well as the sub-conscious, the theory had become standard in hypnotically relaxing one so deeply that the client is sure to bypass the workings of the sub-conscious and to make contact with the superconscious - a spirit guide. That's sort of true but the thing is, now that we're clearing some of the subconscious residue in the basement, that long series of visualizations will combine with failure-anxiety that builds until it drops the vibration of the motivation itself. The surf board the client is riding during this process of hypnosis, at first rises as they begin to relax, and then drops off with the tension of *not getting anything* once the process becomes overly-prolonged. That in itself causes some fear-based results. I, per-sonally, have never had a client lose their conscious awareness during this process – well, wait; a couple have fallen asleep briefly – but basi-cally that is a mistaken belief that I myself thought to be true in my early discovery period – that the conscious mind would somehow step aside and allow a movie to play out on the back of my eyelids. Should the conscious mind actually step aside and allow the guide to speak with-out the client's knowledge – well, that is called trance-channeling and under the circumstances of the regression, the guide doing the speaking is aligned with the tiring-of-the-whole-process *emotional reaction* of the client, whose mind just stepped out due to the fear of failure to get results combined with the stress of the procedure, which will provide material based on that wave of perception/resonance. Don't take that wrong, the guide will provide you with some good information, but be prepared to sort through the subterfuge of the fear, as the fear will be one issue addressed. But that's just my opinion based on the tour of my intuitive self, led by none-other than my invisible entourage.

Spirit guides are always aspects of higher self, true; however, the information you get from any spirit guide is calibrated to match the mo-tivational wave of energy you ride as you approach the big kahuna. It is never a case of a guide not being of a high enough caliber but more that the questions or the motivation of the seeker/channeler may stem from a desire that is overly-distorted by fear, meaning coming more from a point of self-glorification than from a need for guidance or solution. That will mean that the need to reassure self of having some important role in the overall scheme of things - which resulted in a desire to explore one's past lives - will place one on the *"road to redemption as that resonant wave of perception."* Translation: there is at least some rationalization in the request. According to the invisible gang, if you trace the desire for past life identity back to the original kernel of angst that *caused* the desire to form, it will always stem from a feeling of being out of synch with a person or situation in a way that wishes to reinvent self. That particular wave of outlook does not provide the highest point of awareness from which to achieve authentic past life results. In truth, according to guide-speak and at this vibration of mass consciousness, the only time one is taken on the ride of authentic past lives from our level of existence is to shore up a misunderstanding in awareness and that usually happens from the other side, meaning it would take place in the unconscious realms rather than during waking states while being prodded by a second party. At this stage of the game, when we initiate the contact with past lives, there is within us a limiting kernel of fear or we wouldn't desire such a journey. This in and of itself assures us of limited results.

I have to tell you that I can only speak from my own experience and that my experience has come through a very different perceptive window at this point because I am working with those especially sought-after spirit guides as directors during and in understanding the process. Most of us want to know there is something greater out there and this is just one way to shore up the concern that once we cross over, we don't just cease to exist, or get stuck because we can't find the light. We are all making great strides in feeling the higher self connection as we traverse the flushing of the fear and we are all pretty much wondering about our dead aunt Tootie so we are gaining an aspect of assuredness in that area. Kudos to us; now dare we take it a step further?

There is no reason, according to guide-speak, to know any more about the past since it holds too much fear for us to try to relate to our now in a healthier way. Our past lives matter, but not so much right now at this current vibration of mass consciousness and during the flush. Our family-soul-pod has birthed a new and more aware set of aspects of study to send to the realm of physicality this time, but in lives previous they were different aspects with different interests during a different time and space and really wouldn't relate well to us now at all. Not only were aspects of study different, most of the soul sparks of your family-soul-pod were different as well. Not only have some of the soul family members changed but the ones that are still there have evolved in awareness, since evolution continues in the realm of spirit as well as here. Many of the belief systems we cling to as our means of salvation are outdated in that they were handed down to very different waves of resonance where thinking and reasoning had not been developed to the point that ours is in the here and now, and also, at times, living conditions were far more harsh. There is no need to carry specific memories of past lives to this life as they would confuse our reason to be here in this day and age. The desire to connect to a past life usually entails some level of fear in a relationship or in an area of unresolved insecurity. *"We do not resolve these issues with scenes from another dimensional window of activity unless you cannot do so on your own."* And even then they would take you higher in awareness rather than into a radically different vibrational pattern from the past. It is kind of like saying they would take you up a few stairs in ability to understand rather than take you down the street to visit a group of neighbors you really don't know or remember. If I haven't made this clear by now, please allow me to reiterate: we do not come back to work on specific relationships with specific people but to mature our perceptions in and of relationships in general. Higher self can amp up our awareness so that we understand the lines of cause and effect in a split second. That is usually all that is needed unless a being is not of sound reasoning capacity.

What is really at the root of the search is the *"desire to connect with higher self and for that reason we have designed our regressions to progress forward into a communion with higher self and aspects of awareness that can lead one to find their own ways of resolution from within."* A regression moves us backwards. What we're after here is a progression, or upward movement in vibration, so that we can commune with guides of a higher vibration than those tied to past life issues, a.k.a. guides of meandering karmic residue.

After some soul-searching in regards to misrepresenting the truth as-I-see-it, when asked to take someone on an excursion through their magnificent past lives, I now find I only lead the client into the past if instructed to do so by guide-speak. Instead, when a client books a regression, I ask them to consider going upward in vibration to meet their spirit guides and experience their own moment of clarity without my translations. This provides them with a knowing that they are tied to an inner source of guidance that can be used without the intermediary assistance of an outsider. Some are not so sure but most want to give it a go. In cases of skepticism, we first provide a walk through the seeming-past and then move forward in vibration to meet higher self or whatever aspects she sends to represent her. I usually have the client visualize an amethyst table with a group of guides waiting for her to join them. At the time of this writing, every client has been happy with the received results, and from my outside perspective, messages were of a much higher wave of resonance, meaning more philosophical and all-encompassing, than that of guides of karmic residue and scenarios clouded in historical judgments.

As I already mentioned, that long, tedious process of relaxation really isn't necessary anymore, especially with those accustomed to the peace-seeking processes of new wave thinking. I don't have to spend long at all doing the hypnosis-thingie. Usually a couple breath suggestions and a walk through the forest of peace and a quick trip up the tunnel of light and we're good to go. I have had some who were there as soon as I told them where we were going. Our fear-flushing has been more effective than we realize. As we let go of layer after layer of fear-based perceptions and reactions, the road to the superconscious mind is not nearly as difficult to locate. There is even an elevator if we want to make the journey easier. That's the great thing about our minds now, they are more able to move around from a conscious perspective. We can talk with Meander and bring up the maturity level of reasoning in our dream state so that we can use it more to design and build our realities. We can take an amethyst stairway to heaven and commune with higher self long enough to get the gist of what we're trying to accomplish and a possible route to explore if we need it. The possibilities are growing for us on an individual level. As for a planetary level, we will have to wait until enough of us move individually to make that rise in vibration for everybody. It will get there; just hang in there and monitor those thoughts and correct those feelings.

After I began to doubt the validity of past life regression, wouldn't you know there would be a bit of an upsurge in business. When I first pursued this study, it wasn't exactly prolific even as a secondary career choice. After I lost my belief in the premise of visiting a past life, I wrestled with my conscience of highest integrity, a must in holding a love vibration, about how to handle this portion of my work. I finally decided that I would be very honest with the client right there in the beginning, using some remarkable results that past clients had experienced that didn't result in past life footage at all but in current, everyday solutions. Not once did this possibility turn anyone away. But what did happen astounded me. It wasn't anything I could identify the first time, but by the time I had performed three regressions, which I now call spirit-led progressions, I had noticed a new pattern emerging and it was completely in synch with my new-found belief system. My wave of resonance changed and my perception of the results changed to match my new-found beliefs. My perceptive window of the whole process moved up an octave in understanding so my mind geared itself to perceive and to encourage a higher layer of connectedness.

During this transition, the first couple regressions that turned progression had particularly fascinating results. Although I find each session to produce an element of euphoric magic, these two tend to stick in my mind because they represent to me the changes in the level of higher realm connectedness possible as we flush our minds of fear and shift towards more clarity in possibility. Both clients were male and both have a tendency toward wishing to be of service in a healing way. One experienced a priest-type guide implanting jewels in his hands and the other was asked to lay his hands into a rose quartz table that had imprints of hands carved into the surface. When he placed his hands in the indentations, he felt an electrical charge running through is fingers and up through the course of his body. To take you through the symbology of the vision-type experience, their hands represented the desire to give and be of service. Implanting jewels and charging the energy of the hands within rose quartz mittens both indicate a need for and desire for healing in a way that clears them of residue so that they may be of service in a healing way for those around them. I might add here that any desire to be of service carries with it an implied request for self-healing so that one may reach a frequency of connectedness that helping others is possible. And the shifting of our motivations that is evident in these two examples, from I-me-mine to being of service to the group, is the big turn that ultimately lifts our vibration of mass consciousness and provides us with some of those higher realm-type-capabilities. Thus far most of the missing element in manifesting our wants, needs and desires has been the inability to think for the good of the whole.

I really believe reincarnation is more complex than we understand and that is only because we have been given a glimpse of the end-result possibility without understanding how it affects us in the here and now. The soul-aspect thing is not well understood yet but it certainly plays out another facet of the reality of the Akashic recording, the soul history that we haven't completely assimilated into our reincarnational understanding. Our soul aspects change, collectively, meaning the areas of study as well as most of the beings in the soul-pod-family, and we change as well during these morphings into physical beings.

The soul pod itself consists of a group of soul sparks of consciousness, little teeny tiny orbs that are really big beautiful brilliant minds, minds that are capable of so much more than ours in the here and now, minds that are centered on similar interests and frequencies and change within the individual soul structure from time to time, as the physical being explores different aspects of self. Please remember that the pod that is your soul in this life does not consist of the same grouping as the last life. Remember also that in spirit we do not operate as individuals but as groups and that format stays true for us in the physical in that the soul holds the group, but the physical being begins with an individual mindset until the development of the crown chakra is complete. Until

that point, communication with the soul takes place at a more subliminal vibration. And to complicate things just a little more, each spark
of consciousness within your soul pod has its own awareness. During
your life, your Akashic recording consists of the individual recordings
of each soul spark member, so looking at a past life can be looking
at a recording of any member of the soul pod, and such recordings
would include other soul sparks that are not members of your life at
this time. Again, for the sake of simplification, soul sparks are units of
spirit mind. Heavy, I know, so don't try to focus overmuch on it other
than to be aware that who you are is far more complex than we have
understood before now and who we were then would never quite match
up closely with the you of now. And once you're in a higher vibration
of consciousness, not difficult to assimilate at all.

In order to simplify this concept, I have mentioned earlier that I
used to work with another channeler and I ran my questions through
her 'channel' for my answers. During that period, we were told that
we had ten guides working with us on the project. After our guides
separated us so that we would create individual windows of perception,
I asked about the guide personalities I had come to associate with our
combined efforts. I was told that five were from my soul family and five
were from hers and that since we were no longer working together, the
other five guides I had come to know and love were no longer a part of
my higher-self-soul-family. That meant that for that particular project
she and I and all of our involved soul sparks shared an Akashic history,
since each aspect of consciousness has its own Akashic recording. Our
ten higher-self-guiding-soul-sparks had their individual recordings as
well as with each of us and for portions of that time, we were all encap-
sulated in one soul pod of memory.

So the tickler here is this, if you were able to visit my Akasha for
that time period, there would be some confusion for us in the here and
now in separating the strings of ownership as far as identification of
guiding energies, or even soul families. There were times when I pre-
ferred the long and winding versions of her guide-speak rather than the
short and to the point responses of my own. That could create a bit of
a knot in the thread of who's who in the Akashic reference guide. Now

add that scenario to your everyday lives every time you communicate with another and see how confusing it could be if you're feeling too much ownership in regards to your Akashic recording or your personal spirit guide. The truth is in there and it is easy to decode if you're operating from a higher principle in love, but by that point, your feelings of attachment are gone and you are not interested in the Akasha for the same reasons as we are in the here and now. We want to feel good about ourselves and a trip to the court of Romeo Medici as his long lost concubine might just do the trick. But as a more evolved being, we would be more interested in how the court intrigues might affect a girl with the upbringing of a wealthy orphan surrounded by people who only wanted her money. Either way, you're getting a lesson on life in the fear frequency, what changes is our reason to visit the fear. I've said it once and I'll say it again; my Akasha et su Akasha. That's just another reference to that 'we are all one' thing.

I think one of the existing confusions in our understanding of reincarnation is in the overly-used idea that we are tied together via past alliances. There is a belief system out there that if we harmed someone in a past life we are here to correct that relationship. The truth is that once you leave here you return to a frequency of love that is high enough that you instantly understand your position and that of the other and you reflect upon it peacefully. Once you return to the realm of spirit, you no longer experience a relationship from the perspective of an individual at all but from one spark of awareness learning to commune with another spark that may be resonating in desire and intention from a completely different wave of perception. More to the point, at least until we make it through the clearing of the fear, we are better off looking at the relationships in our present life. To look at them in terms of another lifetime fails to honor the relationship of the here and now.

In the end, it's almost like the cartoon of Sam the Sheepdog and Ralph the Wolf; after spending the whole show trying to best each other, they simply punch out at the time clock, shake hands and say goodbye. There is no harm done once in spirit. Because the e-motionating force is of a higher resonance, desires and intentions never seek to harm or to win but to find new aspects of awareness to dig into. That's why incarnating into the lower resonance is appealing for a time, we learn things we would never glean from the higher octaves, plus we still have those lower waves of conflict-based resonance to erase from our Akasha and that does not happen until we all attain complete understandings in cooperation and in always moving for the good of the group. Once we reach that point, that old wave of past history ceases to exist in the Akasha and we are free to move on.

Our earthly concept of justice, or the desire to see someone punished, or to have one suffer as you might have due to the action of another, is revenge and it should not exist in our frame of reference. If someone does us harm, it is because they are unsure of self in a way that causes knee-jerk reactions to protect self without thinking things through. At some point in our fear-flush, we will have released enough of that fear that we begin to consider how those around us are affected by our wants, needs, desires, intentions and actions. When you get to that point, you may still have the occasional 'hhmm, what goes around comes around' thought, but for the most part, you will release the need for come-uppance and will realize that you are taking conscious control of those thoughts and realigning them with a more love-based pattern.

If your father died after having a fight with your brother, there is no need to worry that his last memory was of being hurt or angry. As he traversed the light, he knew immediately that he was mistaken in his perceptions and that your brother's position might have stemmed from a completely different motive than he even realized at the time. He would regain his ability to read the lines of cause and effect and he would be fine with it. He would have risen from the fear-laden vibrations and moved up to a place of love, where all feeling is based in cooperation and compatibility. He doesn't experience negative emotional feelings anymore; the *fear* is gone. He didn't even have to look for the light; that is a natural phenomenon. Interestingly, the tunnel of bright light actually indicates an area of *potential use* when using higher waves of manifestation, something we are not privy to until we ride higher waves of love and have erased the waves of resentment, conflict, revenge, and other such waves of negative emotional current. Non-cooperative influences are considered *doing harm*. This wave of resonance must be cleared before we can access the ON switch for manifestation. Later on, as we clear more of the harmful thoughts and feelings, the tunnel of light will appear when we use our design and build app. It signifies that our manifestation capabilities are in the ON position and the white light is to be used to design your thought matrix, sort of an alive and active blueprint for what you're creating, and an actual depiction of lucid dreaming. Lucid dreaming is taking control of the dream state in that you are consciously calling in the appropriate dimensional doorway to manifest your dream/desire.

So if our past lives left us with karmic areas of resolution, that doesn't mean we have people to atone to. It isn't a person that requires atonement. The point of karma is to bring around a complete under-standing in awareness of the difficulty so that should you find yourself in similar circumstances again, you would never return to said pattern of erroneous feeling, perception or behavior. It isn't the *who* in a relation-ship that is as important from spirit, but here in the physical, relation-ships are lock and key. Because we are operating at a more individual perspective here, relationships are our basic building blocks. Making that move from I-me-mine to the good-of-the-group is instrumental in our evolution and that can only happen through human interaction. Our relationships are sacred, every one. It isn't about finding your friends from past lives but about treating everyone that crosses your path as though they are your friend in this life. When you can do that, you have completed another understanding; another bit of awareness to take with you should you decide to incarnate again. You get to carry more of the old-soul wisdom.

There is another aspect of this belief system evolution that I, as a psychic reader, would really like to address and to do so in this book because when you're here to see me as a client, you are often times too vulnerable for me to explain to you how these things work – at least my truth based on the lessons of guide-speak. We have already discussed spirit guides to some degree. We all have them, starting with Ecknoreial and the buffer zone and the guides of karmic responsibility, and then we have Meander, who is not a guide in the way we think of spirit guidance, but does influence us in the same way. Meander-bluff is there too, usually trying to prove herself by barking up the wrong tree again, but meaning well, nevertheless. Think of Meander-bluff as immature reasoning that requires a good logical consultation with you every once in a while, especially when it's time to discard a pile of reasoning that isn't working for you anymore.

That's a whole lot of guide-speak there in your mind and it really doesn't matter what form they take, in fact, what form they take depends a lot on how you will receive them. Ecknoreial is in charge of cast and costumes and she hands them out judiciously, depending on my awareness of such things. During my work with the other channeler, I had a guide I called Gwyneth. She claimed to be my main spokesperson at the time, which means she represented the wave of resonant energy I was riding at the time of our communications. I found the name Gwyneth to be particularly reassuring since ten years before her acquaintance I had named my car Gwyneth Petrol – I was tired of stopping to pump gas. The resurgence of the name was a sign for me that Gwyneth was the real deal. That's how Ecknoreial works; take some tidbit out of our subconscious and the ring of familiarity will serve to bond you to the accompanying information.

The point I am trying to make here is that your Ecknoreial is the mother of all your guides and they are all roles played by your own soul. If you happen to have an Indian guide named Chief Pumping Gas, that is all well and good but he is still a character casted by your higher self. The truth is, higher self has it all under control up there. Your Ecknoreial doesn't need help from a long lost relative to get the job done. I'm not saying it is impossible for your great aunt Matilda to make contact with you but I am saying there is no need for it and since your Ecknoreial knows exactly what is required for you to reach the goals listed on your blueprint for this life; she is going to monitor things well. Nine out of ten times, according to the invisible faction, you are hearing from the cast of higher self when you think you might be hearing from John Lennon or Elvis' great aunt who was also your fourth cousin once removed from life at least two hundred years prior. Higher self will assign a cast of characters that will provide you with whatever you most need at the time. If it's excitement to create an aura of expectation or reason to understand the actions of one long-passed, your Ecknoreial can make it happen.

That doesn't mean your dear-departed grandmother doesn't still love you and wouldn't love to stop in for coffee some morning when you least expect it, but here's the thing; she isn't your grandmother anymore. When we return to the realm of spirit, we will only hold our incarnated personality/vibration for a short time; just long enough to finish up any unresolved business that grandmother, still with her grandmotherly identity, insists must be completed, and that is usually not very much. As soon as such things are concluded, grandmother re-unites with her soul aspects and they gather for a sabbatical to discuss and explore how things progressed while incarnated. After that point, they resume their spirit identity and resonance, morphing off into aspects unknown for destinations unknown, like hanging with other spirit beings while checking out planets with similar evolutionary patterns of awareness. And as a side note here, relationship attachments exist in our plane of experience. Once returned to her complete vibration as a soul being and no longer subjected to the feeling world of us humans, a visit from grandmother might feel quite impersonal and could even cause hurt feelings since our need for connection to a loved-one is so strong. For that reason, it is a more pleasant experience if higher self orchestrates and scripts the visits from our dear departed loved ones.

"Does this make sense?" If you've ever had a reading from me, you will have heard this phrase before. I can't help it; I am not even sure if I am the one asking. It usually pops out after a short channeled synopsis and it gives me time to recoup my own thoughts as well as answer questions before I forget what was said. But does it make sense yet? As a spirit spark, we have unlimited potential and can do about anything that we come up with as far as ideas, but here in the physical, and especially on this planet at this time, we are somewhat quarantined in what we can and cannot do. This is partially because our vibration of mass consciousness is so vulnerable and partially because we are in a process of clearing fear to lift the veil of physical consciousness to a higher degree of awareness. In all truth, it is probably not your grandmother following you around and waiting for you to smoke up the place so you can see her, it is more likely your higher self pointing out where you are in terms of thoughts and verbalizations so that you can move forward in resonance. Hanging with past-patterns keeps you stuck.

We are vulnerable and easily deluded because our fears keep us from experiencing life at its fullest potential. We are searching for spirit and depend too much on that influence because we have yet to understand that we are capable of creating our divine existence ourselves and right here from this slower dimension of reality. Ok, so not quite yet, but we're getting there. It is one of the long term goals. What we need to know is that we are always connected to a higher source of guidance and possibility, and we will know that once we have flushed enough fear that the fog begins to clear.

I want to know what *new* fields of study we can explore – so I am asking...

And we are speaking.

CHAPTER 8

MY ELLIPTICAL STAIRWAY TO HEAVEN

There is a set of evolving guidelines used by our soul guidance and the higher realms in regards to the care and fueling of the physical species. That missive is referred to in some legends as the Ark of the Covenant.

"The Ark of the Covenant has been expanded and expounded upon since it first made its appearance as a blueprint in the design and keeping of our species' physical well-being. Upon the realization that our incarnating sparks of awareness were too young in development to handle the responsibility of mind-based manifestation, the upper valves of creation were dismantled until the being displayed a maturity level capable of mastering the elements as well as exploring his or her unique set of desires and beliefs. This has not yet happened with your species. In the case of most other planets involving a dimension of physical experience, the upper awareness valves are in the ON position so that the species can learn to use their conscious awareness for more than meeting survival needs, an unfortunate result of the OFF position during our existence here on Earth, something that came to be due to the rise of a concept very seldom even discovered on most planets – conflict."

We didn't start it; we were born into it, but we have yet to resolve it.

We are truly a race of explorers in that our unique circumstances lend a new level of possibility in understanding how the more dense energies behave when fear, the catalyst that lends energy that boomeranging path of movement, opens doorways. Our experience of gravity is unique in its magnetic hold on us and the airwaves that hold our internet and our favorite reality TV show in check. When the movement of energy is directed by a higher degree of love, it is expansive and moves quickly in the direction targeted by its sender, but in your case, when coupled with the element of fear, your thoughts, which are your creative-directives, take on a self-magnetized curve and come back at you in the form of gravitational pull.

Think of fear as a case of feeling overly-self-centered and that will begin to make sense. If our focus stays too close to self and self's considerations, the energy is unable to flow in a connective way to possible creative endeavors. It simply cannot move far enough outwards to get past creating a very central center of gravity – around me and my bathroom scale if that is where my focus tends to be.

Indeed; electrical current is heavily utilized in the here and now as it exemplifies the arc of possibility when the mind's directives are still in the hold position. Gravity is stronger on this planet than most but will ease up, as will the need for electronic devices, once we open our minds to the greater possibility, and once we cease to do harm in even our quietest thoughts.

In addition to our project of realigning the subconscious with a higher frequency of love, another chapter has been added to our Covenant now in that a new dimensional doorway was opened about four to five years ago. Up until that point, several techniques had been tried and discarded as far as how to best complete the physical journey and return to the land of spirit – our doorway to even higher realms. The first stop now is and has been, since the initiation of the Covenant, to reside for a time with the guiding family of one's soul. There were times when that was not as effective as desired in terms of restoring awareness to its original condition since some of the elements of fear remained in said being's outlook. For that reason, we initiated a type of shower of love where we discuss and resume a play out of circumstances from a seemingly-physical realm until a level of awareness is achieved so that the fear can be disseminated. At that point, said being would return to a level of love high enough to enjoy his original format of existence and move on from there until called to return to the physical in attempt to clarify and condition any incomplete understandings, thereby clearing any personal karmic residue that holds the planet in a magnetic state. That in-between state was not a ghost-like existence but more a play-off of what had happened – it took place within the Akashic recording.

The ideas of ghosts are actually an attempt on our part to condition your thinking to a point of realizing that your thoughts do harm when internalized in a state of misery. There's that filing system we talked about earlier. Most ghost legends are ones of sadness or anger and will mesmerize those in need of healing in similar areas. It is we who cause you to see the apparitions and we who cause the noises and running water sounds that hold your thoughts mesmerized while we clean the portals of discord within. You are easily hypnotized when you think there might be a spirit being in your midst.

The newer method involves an automatic transferal of mind to an identical-appearing staging area of the being's physical life. All roles are now played by the soul family, who will mimic the ideals and personalities of the original cast of characters. The main difference here is that the being will learn to take responsibility for his or her thoughts, words and actions based on a unique format in that all decisions this one makes and utilizes will stem from self.

The accompanying personalities will suddenly take opposition only when the thinking process requires alleviation of fear in some area that is requiring completion. Once the being achieves a sufficient amount of awareness in the required areas that they can begin to plan a corrective procedure, they return to the spirit realm equipped to resolve as much of their karmic residue as possible from the higher realm. This requires some adjustment in your thinking in that we are not helping you to live your lives but to make sound decisions based on the good of the whole.

(Already knowing about this new dimension and also noticing that my husband was actually agreeing with me more often than not, I found myself asking the air over my head if I had already died and just didn't know it...)

Joking aside, guide speak translations are not as necessary as they were in the beginning of this book because I am managing to stay in a higher frequency where some layers of distortion have disintegrated. In this particular case, while they were talking my mind wandered into a question of *what is happening when we cross over?* Some of their answers to clients seeking word from long, lost loved ones was sparking a new layer of curiosity within me. As you can see, since my focus shifted from the ark of the covenant to this new topic, my self-us-superconscious-mind realigned with my conscious awareness; a point to consider when listening for the voice of the higher realms. And as the fear-flush makes progress, a quiet, receptive state of mind becomes more normal.

The symbolism that became a design of higher awareness is now a lesser requirement in that I can see my areas of distortion more quickly and realign to get an easier answer from the invisible gang. There are times when I use the final outcomes as my beginnings to explore my new awareness and times when I hear my voice within command my attention at just the right time. This gentle leading guidance is always present without the voice of conviction nor with the sense of importance attached to any one being, thing or circumstance. I have come to realize that whatever life produces becomes manageable once I believe and know I can find my inner voice of wisdom, should I require help. There are times when I wish for something new to wear or something new to write and I find that I need to take the action to get there, and if necessary, ask for an easy button. What I am trying to say is this: the spiritual search has lost its intensity. My focus has shifted from that of seeking my spiritual friends in this life to that of finding the right way to make life easy and workable with those in my immediate areas of life. The spiritual search started when I wanted to find a way to fit in and the search ended when I realized that how I fit in wasn't nearly as important as is how we all function as a whole. My over-focus on self is slowly beginning to dissipate.

I think my most recent swirly is almost over. I have spent the last six weeks in different cycles of wash, rinse, and repeat until I am beginning to feel that *new dawn on the horizon* feeling. During this laundering of my fear-based perceptions, I felt great discomfort in my lower extremities. Upon arising from bed in the morning or just from a chair in the afternoon, I had to pick my legs and feet up just to get them to cooperate in a normal fashion. A lot of root charka discord that would probably have awarded me an arthritis diagnosis if I had visited the doctor, but I knew it was flush-related so I ignored it and went about my business. Guide-speak and I discuss these things as they are happening and even though I don't know which issues are septic-bound, I do know when I am caught in a loop of clearing, which means a loop of healing will soon follow.

As I agitated through the wash cycle again, I was hyper-aware of how pathetic I looked when I stood up to walk. My lower body was so stiff and uncomfortable that I considered having an elevator installed in the foyer. I couldn't be barefoot and walk well; it felt like I was walking on bare bones and sore bare bones at that. The awkward stiffness would only take about fifteen seconds to auto-correct but I was overly self-conscious until then.

After I moved out of my self-centered phase and began to look around me, I noticed people all over walking as gingerly as I was, even kids. I began to relax again as I realized that maybe I am not ready for a walker, just making my way through the particles of disintegrating beliefs that have held me captive to sights, sounds and smells somewhere below where I want to be. I would ask if I should see the doctor and would hear that small voice within that just said, *ignore it.* That quiet little thought stayed consistent throughout the emotional roller coaster ride that comes free with every swirly. It confirmed for me that my physical impairment was temporary.

Then one morning I woke up without physical discomfort. I got moving right away and didn't require a warm-up period if I sat down. I noticed I was hyper-aware of things in need of doing so *I got my cleaning rags out and put my glad rags away for another day.* (yes, that was them, talking like an old lady so I know it had something to do with purging old stuff...) By the time I went to bed, I had accomplished a lot more than I had for several weeks. It felt good to be back on track again.

But now it is a few days later and I have to say, I *thought* my swirly was over, and maybe a personal portion of it was, but it's beginning to look like the whole fam-damily just got plopped into the pre-soak cycle of the wash. Instead of finding our own personal paths of newness, we are working again on finding a common pattern of communication as well as existence that blends well with all here in this house and immediate family extensions. It's a good thing I got some cleaning done or I would be wallowing in a messy nest too. Do you ever feel like you just cleaned up one tree when another falls across your path? That's how it is when you're being slowed up so you can change your M.O.

*"Let's just say we're slowing you up again until you find your measure of worth in what you are **not** doing rather than what you are doing..."*

Quick translation; basically, they are referring to our repatterning. We train our raw emotional reactions to rise upwards in maturity when we resist the urge to follow our old, less mature patterns. For instance, all too often we stake our identity claim on our job/career or whatever project we're wrapped up with at the moment. Finding our measure of worth in what we are not doing entails realizing that we're no longer reacting in the old fear-stained mode, but finding a new level of self-recognized and self-actualized progress, just because we are alive and because we care enough about those around us to put them first more than once in a while.

"It is not the book that has the value; it is your mind."
??

The question marks were me. They typed the line in here about a week ago and I went on with my discourse and forgot about it. As I came face to face with it again, I had no idea what they were telling me so I shut the computer off and went to bed. I had a very busy day coming up and frankly, wasn't sure if I should try to decode it or just erase it.

So I had my busy day, all without incident or frustration, and even wrapped things up slightly before another trip to the airport to retrieve my husband. I laid on the couch for a few just to resolve and regroup – and check for pinholes in my eyelids. There was some definite resolving going on, meaning the dream state was beginning to materialize while I was awake enough to provide a level of emotional reasoning beyond that of Meander, and then I began to relax. The next thing I knew I was listening to a voice again, only this time it said something about it not being the book that was important, it was my mind. And then the book began to write itself - Finally!

The guiding voice took me back about twenty years ago. I had a vision just as I finished meditating, something I don't seem to require as much these days in terms of stress management but do require in terms of finding the opening for my creative efforts. On this particular day, as I finished, I walked through the dining room, where, for a brief moment, I had a very life-like vision of a tiny, little old lady sitting at the end of the table. She was so small that she might have been about the size of an elf, but more fairy-like in her physical build; small-boned and thin, unlike moi. She had gray, grandma-permed hair and a calico blouse with a gray background and tiny red floral print. I seem to remember the fabric from somewhere in the 60s or 70s. She looked at me and said, *"my name is Selvis, remember that!"* I remember trying to make a mental note of the name and, as if reading my mind, she said, *"yes, do it that way then, remember Elvis with an S."*

I was quite fascinated with Selvis and searched for all kinds of hidden meanings in her appearance and what she wanted to tell me. I imagined her being behind all the mysteries I created in my mind to make my life more interesting; i.e., taking the focus off the complexities of my world. I had a couple earth-mother type friends who were quite sure that her appearance was to make sure I spent more time outside as I tend to prefer my house. I had mixed feelings about that but did take to the backyard more. Finally I forgot about Selvis and moved on with my life but as I lay on the couch that busy day, the voice said, *"remember Selvis.....the book is about Seflus, your mind....Self –Us. Self equals Us."*

That's it! That's what I am trying to say in this book – that as we shift our focus to the good of the group, our minds are moving from self to a conscious connection with our Ecknoreial groups and with our Meanders – Self becomes Us in that we are gaining at least two more heads when it comes to using the one attached to our shoulders. And although too new to talk about, I am also beginning to communicate with the mind of my body. That's where *Iotta* comes in, but communication with her is too new for me to discuss just yet. She will be another member of the Self-Us team but one that will not speak much in this book because I have not learned to line that consciousness up with that of my still maturing mind. I have to reach a point of unconditional love, give or take a few degrees, from my conscious heart-mind before I have direct access to the body-mind, but just so you know: that is the beginning of self-healing, regenerating body parts and reprogramming our present body tendencies, i.e., changing genetics. Right now the invisible faction does the work for me but I have to assume the role of driver here right quick or they'll just let me itch away my life force on small irritations.

I am beginning to see why some of the things our soul families put us through right now are misunderstood, but suffice it to say this, many of our beliefs about spirit and how things operate from the higher realms are analogies designed to help us begin to understand that there is more out there beyond the perception of our five senses. Some of the material was simplified so we could better understand it and some has been misconstrued down through the ages. We are reaching a point in awareness where we need to understand things better than we do if we plan to release some of the fear from our belief systems, and that's what it takes to raise the vibration of mass consciousness. I don't mean to sound like a naysayer, debunking your favorite TV shows and the like, but it is time we put some of our old reference materials in the museum and begin to think for ourselves. Make of that statement what you will. The past hasn't served us all that well and the future requires something beyond what we have heretofore experienced. The truth is out there and has always been out there in limited doses, but our efforts to make it more understandable have resulted in descriptions and understandings that fall short of the truths we are now beginning to access from within our own conscious awareness.

Once you reach a point in love-based perceptions that you can begin the path of taking conscious control of your life, there is no need to search for the secret doors. You make the choices and are secure in the belief that higher soul will be there to assist as necessary. Although there are some parameters set up in our life-blueprints before we get here, mostly which aspects of awareness we will work with during this life, the primary conditions are usually the natural result of what is occurring all around you. Higher Soul gets involved when there is need for tweaking. Had we discovered this earlier, we wouldn't have spent so much time searching for the perfect career, we would have already defined ourselves in terms of much simpler data: *Hello, I am Rhonda and I am here to discover who I am by learning how I can hold myself in an unconditionally loving state no matter the circumstances. How may I be of service?*

The search for signs comes with an easier button than we think. The need to translate every natural incident in life in terms of self is one idea that will tend to recede as we learn that we are natural products of the life streams of our community. One morning on my way out the door I counted twenty-two turkeys pecking around in my backyard. Never having noticed them before, the sudden appearance of twenty-two turkeys seemed somehow a magic indication of significance. After perusing all my magical-sign-translating-wisdom, I asked my entourage if there was any message for me in the flock clustered around the backyard hickory tree. Guide-speak had spent a lot of time showing me how they can make sure we see what they want us to see and that what they show us isn't always the real truth but has a cause that, at that moment in time, is aligned with our personal frequency. As I backed out of the drive and started down the street they said, "*the turkeys aren't a sign, they are always there; If we want you to see a sign, we would do this...*" and suddenly I was aware of a tree limb off to the side of the road where a giant brown bird took flight towards my windshield, but just before it hit, it disappeared. I silently asked what bird it was and they said, "*an eagle.*" It indeed fit the description but I didn't realize they were so big.

"*They are.*"

Wow; then I asked if it was real, not immediately comprehending that there were no trees along that portion of the street, and they said, "*No.*" The bird was a vision that looked so real I probably would have argued with anyone in the car who missed the near-miss to my windshield. They will use these guide-illustrating visions to lift us off the wrong wave of energy from time to time, but that doesn't make the magical incident a prophesy nor should it be used forever as a rule in navigating your life. Since guides are usually interested in our emotional *creations,* they are usually alerting us to the sounds and songs in our thoughts and feeling centers. Throw that bad vibe thing out the window; it is saying you are riding the wrong surf-wave again.

Recently I was having a hard time getting off the what's-wrong-with-me-train and I asked Ecknoreial for help in lifting me up. I was kitchen-cleaning – AGAIN – which was really doing nothing to help my stuck-in-the-mud attitude. I glanced out the window at the woods and noticed a wild bush that seemed to have unusually large leaves, something I had never noticed before, when I heard them tell me to look again. I glanced back at the bush and the large leaves were now huge white flowers, like plate-sized hibiscus blooms. I am no gardener but I know there were no flowers out there before. As I stood entranced by the beauty of the huge white blooms they explained that *Our Lady of Illumination* had simply refracted a little sunlight to make the leaves appear white. Mission accomplished. I was feeling connected again and able to make the next train out of grumpy-land not only from seeing a little magic, but had I missed that part, just the beauty of the flowers would have helped raise the reading on my love barometer.

Learning to recognize where I am on the barometer of love has been the biggest lesson of the fear flush. I had artistically wound myself into a chain of mail so protective and faddishly glimmering that I lost sight of the vulnerable puff ball hiding inside my suit of armor. No longer governed by whatever trend speaks to me of being the best me that I can be, I am now able to recognize a good deal of the fear and am learning to curtail the fear-based thoughts and realign with a higher wave of insight before my random thought takes flight and creates a whiff of whatever I don't want. That is the missing piece in our ability to manifest. Our desires and our motivations are misaligned because they are tied to our defense mechanisms, which allows our fear of not having enough, or of not being good enough, to continue to refuel the negativity. Once our pursuits are coming from a place of *do no harm* and *for the good of all*, we can set our sights on something greater than just paying the bills and choosing a career. Imagine a world where you envision movement to other worlds to explore greater possibility than just *what's for dinner?* We all want something more but our ideas of what is possible have been squelched until we can shave off the old restrictions that come with our fear-based dogmas; it is then that we can move into a world of super-hero possibility without need of saving anyone; with the knowing that we all really save ourselves.

"We are now learning to use our voices in our upward development of vibration and we are also able to hear our guide-speaks, which indicates that we are moving forward in vibration, but we are also knowing that we are not there yet and that we are never going to get there listening to our guides speak..."

Very cute, but yes, they're speaking for me but it really isn't necessary. The key here is that the guides are not here to provide us with entertainment nor with proof of their existence anymore unless we really need it. They are here to let us know we've reached the apex of the crown chakra where we, as the *Lower yet Ascending Self*, are now in conscious awareness of our Higher Self. It is like saying the Ascending Self, the physical me, has finally met the Higher Self, my soul guidance, the watchers that guard the gateway to the higher possibilities of my Rhonda-Mind. At that point, Ascending Self learns to take the controls of our creative forces and bring Higher Self in for clarity of purpose and direction or for solution-based thinking. We are soon to learn to manage the elements and the bursts of bad weather on our own rather than to passively seek signs that point us to an area of safety.

"Yes, you are moving up the chakra chain in development but you know you cannot depend on us as a means of discovery due to the fact that you are learning to discover on your own. We can point you and we do."

And yet another keyboard hijacking...

Woops again; Correction per the invisible faction: this is really not a keyboard hijacking but a *"non-hostile takeover of my verbiage,"* per the all-wise and knowing ones. Alright, this further illustrates my point. My choice of words is important in the overall study of love frequencies; I should not refer to them as hijackers but I can count on them to provide magic and insight when actually needed, not as fuel for my all-too-easily-regenerating ego, but when my most basic desires stem from a wave of emotion, the food-stuffs of motivation, and an integral part of our intention, to be of service to the whole.

In thinking of how this invisible mind I call my guides seems to work magically with me in terms of pointing me in the direction I seek, my thoughts meandered towards some of our recent inclement weather patterns. Is it a shifting of the earth and her positioning or is there more to it? Can we really manage the weather and speak with the elements that make up all aspects of our mothering planet? Considering this, cleaning up our minds will allow us to finally learn to use some of those multi-dimensional talents we have been seeking through all our legends of dragons and unicorns and captive princesses and knights of holy grails. *We wanna' do it too-oo*. And it turns out there is a very good reason why; that desire is the very basis of our divine blueprint. Once upon a time we set out to learn to operate here in the physical realm with the same degree of multidimensional capability as we hold when we are our spirit-self. Can we get there from here?

It turns out that on other planets where the vibration of mass consciousness is high enough to leave our capability of manifestation in the ON position, it is quite normal to get there and get there quickly. We're still working on it. We took the remedial classes, knowing it was the long way home but would provide deeper insights for plans that come later in our personal evolutions. It is because we're requiring divine assistance in our ascension, that caused me to consider that this roller-coaster ride we're on now was an experiment that had failed. But I am also realizing that if that were the case, if we were finished with the study of our physical world, what would the point be in the divine intercession? We have much yet to learn and we're really not here only because of karma in the most common understanding of the term. We really don't have to pay back every iota of harm we've ever projected, just understand the error of our ways. We are healing those unresolved karma-bank balances as we go, with every layer of fear we resolve and with every behavior we successfully repattern in love. At this point we need simply to complete the understanding necessary to keep from making the same mistakes again, not to pay off past-life mortgages.

Karma is just a time-delay in clearing the harmful energy we stir up while we're here, but clearing our personal harmful energy really takes place quite naturally as we move back up into the realm of spirit, where we all reside in our normal state, one of love and peace and for the good of the whole. It is true, however, that we left this planet our imprint, not in terms of carbon usage but as our personal contribution to the planetary magnetic grid, which is made up of our belief systems and waves of emotion. That is the energy field that holds our vibration of mass consciousness in place. That is what we're working to change now. That is where we are on this planet at this juncture in time, but it is important to remember that spirit is also a realm of evolution and things will change there as well in order to meet the needs of the present. So we're really not heading for an end of times so much as a rebirthing of our consciousness while here in the physical.

As I wafted over this subject matter I was impressed to head up-stairs to my other computer and grab the file on an upcoming workshop. I felt like I needed a quick peek-through of the material just in case I needed some refreshing. As I opened my document file, I saw a folder I really didn't remember and felt the urge to press the open button. Inside was a subheading entitled *Chakras 8 through 12*. A long time ago I dug around in various interpretations of chakras pertaining to an ascended state of consciousness but I put the interest away with the feeling that the material felt too far from my reality to hold much weight with me. This time I looked again at the descriptions and heard, *"this is what you are talking about right now."*

Sure enough, most of the concepts that I have been trying to explain in this book and in my workshops were right there, as plain as day. My understanding of the higher chakras wasn't even hitting the light of day the last time I tried to understand them and now they are a part of my reality, even if I know I have to employ the assistance of the buffer zone and the help of a higher soul to make it all happen. I have been describing our consciousness evolution in terms of the first seven chakras, but there was as much going on above that, in regards to our mind's expansion, as within the first seven. There was even mention of the *clearing of the fear*, the confirmation I needed for my swirly-theory. The invisible faction mentioned something about traveling up the chakra chain earlier in this chapter and I thought I knew what they meant, but it turns out there was another whole layer on top of that statement. I had to rise up a couple more stairs to get the additional understanding. Now I have the answers to some of the questions I am working through. It seems these superhero abilities that I keep seeking ways to tap into are right there in my ability-blueprint, I just have to reach the level of awareness that comes quite naturally with mental and emotional maturity. I can honestly say that higher self will provide answers if you ask for them. I look through a metaphysical window and that is how they present my new material and make the connections for me that don't seem to add up once I begin to think outside the box again. We all have our own personal windows of perception and that is how our soul families will package our newly matured concepts and bonus material. I can see, now, how well constructed the clues were that led me back to this obscure file of information that I really don't remember ever seeing or saving in the first place.

So to clear up what I have talked about thus far on my stairway to heaven, it seems that all things *are* possible from *the physical plane*, which is also called *the world of form* in some of the ancient teachings. As our subconscious realigns with a higher degree of emotional maturity, we will be able to clean our water and environmental conditions with our minds. The complication in our realm of possibility is that our vibration of mass consciousness has dropped lower than normal and was allowed to continue at that lower wave to see if we could overcome the negative-based outlooks without divine assistance. As I understand it now, we do overcome the lower resonance at a personal level, but that can take us on a twenty to thirty-thousand-year sojourn. We will start a journey as an elemental, a single unit of one of the elements of this amazing planet, where we learn to hold form first, such as the form of a tiny drop of rain. We move on to the plant kingdom and the animal kingdom, doing our perfunctory stints as the body, the mind and the soul of each life-species. The journey will continue until each of us learns to navigate as the mind of the human species from a vibration high enough to no longer require the special layering of soul guidance.

As the mind of the human, we will actually operate from the physical plane with a high enough level of awareness that we assume the vibration of the soul and commune as needed with the even-higher realm beings that our soul members use as mentors. We will move even beyond that layer of advanced awareness until we can assume the role of creator god, or maybe that of a planet, or maybe even hold the position of the mind of the central sun of a universe. There will come a point where we choose whether or not we wish to continue in the physical realm, or move onto other avenues of evolution; for instance, I don't think we choose to hold the form of body, mind or soul-guidance of a planet or sun from this physical realm, but from higher realms than my mind can conceive on this day. We can, however, just like our own fore-fathers, create our own species from this world of form. But now I am having more questions, like how many worlds of form are possible and what different things can we do at these differing junctures in our mind's development?

But where are we in the here and now? Just about to access the connection to the higher realms on a conscious basis so that we can learn to assume the role of our soul guidance while still acting as the mind of the human being. Simply put, a layer of additional guidance was inserted when the species was still young, too young to manage a true maturing of mind evolution when learning in an environment where the vibration of mass consciousness was allowed to hold a greater percentage of fear than usual. The original plan was to allow a spark of consciousness to assume the role of the mind of the human while maintaining powers of creation and also carrying conscious connection to the higher realm layers of mentoring. Once it was determined that the vibration of mass consciousness was limiting the understanding of the evolving human mind, an additional layer of mentorship was added to the mix, the layer of soul, while the powers of creation were dismantled until the rise in mass consciousness, where the human mind would reach a vibration high enough to communicate consciously with the soul layer. Next, the human mind will progress to take the role of soul guidance as part of its normal conscious makeup.

That is where we are now, learning to take conscious control of our physical package, which includes lining up the various minds within this body we call home. Oh, and by the way, until we are ready to assume the role currently played by our soul energy; we will practice as members of soul pods during our spirit-realm stints. So I guess I finally understand where soul energy comes from.

The fear-flush, or subconscious realignment as it is being called out in the channeling ethers right now, is part of the opening of the third eye, where your body consciousness enters the world of your conscious mind. It opens the doorway so you can actually watch your errant feelings and reasoning open an old wound and bleed a little every time your mind wanders down an old path of grief. It helps you learn in a hurry exactly how to realign that subconscious reasoning so the wound will finally close for good. This new alliance with your body-mind will eventually take you to self-healing, which goes a good deal farther than just healing the sniffles. We will soon see body parts regenerating with the right circumstances in mind-development.

A couple months ago I noticed a small blood-blister on the back of my ring finger. It would appear I had somehow pinched a nerve in my mind, for lack of better explanation. I noticed that during certain times of the day, the spot would bleed, not stopping until I bandaged it to avoid blood stains on carpeting, clothes and whatever else I might need to see clean and flawless...

After a month or so the small spot had become an open wound and would eventually morph into a tumescent growth that I kept well under cover lest my overly-observant husband press me to see a doctor. I knew the process; swirly in progress. The subconscious realm would benefit from my discomfort of the situation; it would be used in the dream state by the guides as they use the quietly swirling kernel of fear to stop a certain emotional reaction down in Meander-land. Up here in the Rhonda-world, the gently percolating fears were used to slow my mind enough to take note of errant thoughts and reasoning. And to be perfectly honest, towards the end of the life of that wayward-growing part of me, I had made peace with seeing the doctor to have it taken off; it was beginning to creep me out more than I care to acknowledge. Then, finally, I managed to have the correct emotional attachment to my new body-part, and I said in the correct, non-reactive way, *I would like to see this heal,* and it did. Right there under my nose, the growth released itself and left a good sized crater in my finger. I made sure my brother saw it so I could have a witness later, plus, I still like to gross him out. Later that day I said again I would like to see it healed completely and as I ran some water over the hole, a fuzzy light seemed to mar my view of the finger and then the hole was gone! The whole process may have taken about five seconds. I asked why I couldn't see it heal and they explained that the healing took place a few degrees above the vibration of my reality so all that I could see was a veil of light.

That's where we're going with this. We are learning to tap into our self-centered feelings and thoughts and correct them so that our bodies can heal themselves, so that our mind can continue to explore new and exciting avenues of possibility and so that we can clean up our planet with the blink of an eye. We're getting there. We really are! Every time I do a workshop I am amazed at how easily the participants pick up on new concepts; concepts that were alien to our normal awareness package just a couple years ago. I am no different than anyone else in terms of immature emotional urgings, but the swirly process has actually helped us clean up our old negative patterns enough that we're making more headway than we know.

Our lower vibration of mass consciousness was an experiment whose time is now ending and so the divine intercession of clearing the fear, which amounts to a premature opening of the third eye along with the crown chakra, is being employed to correct the lower resonance of energy in the here and now. Normally we wouldn't experience the clearing of the fear with as much bleed-through because we would have been further along in our ability to hold our love meters up there. That is one of the pitfalls of our unusual situation. But we're getting there. The fear-flush and resulting inner dimensional shift that we're all experiencing right now is kind of like moving from AM to FM radio in frequency, but now we have the possibility of even moving to Sirius radio, where we can choose the channel we most resonate with until we create one of our own. We're slowly activating chakras eight through twelve and adding some of our superhero capabilities to our Clark Kent persona. Maybe someday soon I'll blow on that wick and light the candle after all.

Oh! And there is this being up there in my soul pod calling himself, at least for today, Raziel; he promised to show me his notebook.

ABOUT THE AUTHOR – RHONDA RHOSE

R honda Rhose-Biritz is an Intuitive Consultant with over twenty years in psychic readings that focus on the healing of the heart and mind and over forty years in the study of metaphysics. The author has the ability to hear her soul-guides at will. They provide personal insight into a client's circumstances in a way that has earned her readings a solid reputation with results known to facilitate growth and forward movement. For the last ten years, interaction with her invisible entourage has been in touring our evolving minds and understanding a process of guidance used by our spirit-based partners in clearing emotional immaturity, a type of fear-flush that is a necessity in opening doorways to higher possibility, to the magic of our legends and lore, the secret desire behind our desires. She has explored her theory of *subconscious fear flush* through hundreds of readings and her work in relaying the information has been well accepted and touted locally, as well as her ability to soothe the anxiety-ridden, sleeplessly hyper-sensitive beings that are immersed in the process. Rhose's private, spirit-led lessons place special focus on identifying the symbolic truth in guide-speak material. Adding to that her twelve years as the *channeling editor* during a stint as channeling duo, Saga-*Rhose*, she has learned well the nuances of *guide-speak*. Translating material from the higher realms is tantamount in gauging when we are bringing in highest truth and when we are subconsciously resolving our negative experiences (*hearing whatever will make us feel better.*) Her understandings of the mind, both the subconscious and the superconscious connection to the higher realm, and her ability to pass that information along in an easy-to-comprehend format lend new dimensions to Rhose's label as that of *psychic*.

www.rhonda-rhose.com

CPSIA information can be obtained
at www.ICGtesting.com
Printed in the USA
FFOW05n2152201116

9 781595 945983